PREDICT MARKET SWINGS WITH TECHNICAL ANALYSIS

PREDICT MARKET SWINGS WITH TECHNICAL ANALYSIS

Michael McDonald

John Wiley & Sons, Inc.

Published by John Wiley & Sons, Inc., New York.
Published simultaneously in Canada.

This publication is designed to provide accurate and authoritative information in
regard to the subject matter covered. It is sold with the understanding that the
publisher is not engaged in rendering professional services. If professional advice or
other expert assistance is required, the services of a competent professional person
should be sought.

ISBN: 0-471-20596-6

Printed in the United States of America.
10 9 8 7 6 5 4 3 2 1

To my good friend and mentor,
the late George O'Brien

Contents

Introduction

THE BEGINNING

Adults often view their lives as somehow planned beforehand. What originally seemed to be unrelated life decisions, like pieces of a jigsaw puzzle, all came together to form a coherent story. My life seems that way to me now.

My first passion was the study of mathematics and physics. From the age of 14, at every Christmas, my parents bought me advanced books on these subjects. From these, I taught myself calculus and Einstein's relativity theories by the age of 15. From this I learned a valuable lesson while relatively young: I found that if I applied myself, I could master complicated subjects on my own.

The first time I became curious about stock investing came while I followed another passion—sports—as a teenager. Back in the early 1960s, the *Los Angeles Times* didn't have a separate section for business; investing and business information occupied the back pages of the sports section. As a teenager I read the sports pages every day.

Because of the newspaper's format, it was inevitable that I would turn the last page on sports and come face to face with business pages containing nothing but numbers. Although I had no interest in investing at the time and didn't understand what the numbers represented, I do remember thinking that some day I would have to study this. If making money was simply predicting what these numbers would be, I could learn how to do it. It would take 10 years before I put that optimistic thought to the test.

I remember the day I started my study of the stock market—August 15, 1971. It was a Sunday evening and President Nixon gave his famous "wage and price controls" speech on television. I only remember him talking about the control of prices and wages, but there was apparently a lot more to his speech. He also shut the gold window on the redemption of U.S. dollars and started the modern currency markets as he floated the dollar free of the fixed exchange rates determined by the Bretton Woods meeting held right after WWII. This I came to understand only later.

The next day, I turned on the television and saw the Dow Jones close up over 30 points on 30 million shares—at that time the biggest point advance on the largest volume ever. Like the starting gun of a race, that moment kicked off an intense interest in the stock market that has continued to this day.

It is debatable whether this was the best point for a young man to begin a study of the stock market. For the next 11 years, the market went essentially nowhere; 2-year bull markets were followed by 1- to 2-year bear markets. By 1978, stocks had become very unpopular investments. No doubt, these early years helped me formulate certain views on investing that I still hold today. These influential years were the reason I never agreed with the now popular buy-and-hold investment philosophy and why I still believe that timing the market is the preferable course.

How to Start?

How does one start a study of the stock market? I started by spending almost every Saturday for 2 years at the Los Angeles Library digging up everything I could find on the subject. I pored over every relevant government publication, reference book, and investment book in the stacks. A number of books started me off in the right direction. The first was the *The Stock Market Profile—How to Invest with the Primary Trend* by Jacobs. This gave me my first lesson in the subject of technical analysis. The second was a book by William X. Scheinman, *Why Most Investors Are Mostly Wrong Most of the Time*, which gave me a firm grounding in the theory of contrary opinion.

I approached this study with an open mind and decided that I would not go down the logical or obvious course. I was too familiar with physics theories that, while true, were based on ideas not at all self-evident, such as the quantum and relativity theories. I didn't limit my thinking only to ideas that seemed logical or obvious. If an idea worked—meaning that you could have predicted the direction of stock prices with it—even if it was strange, it still came under consideration.

I had already determined that I should study the overall stock market rather than focusing on individual stocks. If stock prices were predictable, that predictability would lie in determining the direction of the whole market rather than that of individual stocks. This decision set me off on the path of studying how to predict the whole stock market rather than individual stocks.

The first project was to discover whether economic information about the state of the economy or various parts of the economy could be used to forecast the stock market. The question posed was, "Is there an economic series, such as housing starts or unemployment, that could have been used over the last 40 years to predict what stock prices eventually did?" You might think that such a study would be very long and detailed, but it wasn't. Since I was looking for something that would be reliable (that is, you could confidently invest money on it), any correlation would have to be obvious and easy to see—it wouldn't be something subtle. These initial studies were therefore very visual in nature. I took 40-year charts of all the economic statistics that economists calculate and overlaid each on top of the chart of the stock market. I was looking only to see if any of these measures consistently dipped or dived before stock prices dipped or dived.

I was assisted in this study by economists' preliminary work on classifying economic indicators into three broad time categories. In a business cycle, not everything happens at the same time; some economic measures come alive early, while others lag behind. Based on this concept, economists classified economic measures using their time sequencing. Indicators are classified as leading, coincidental, or lagging indicators. *Coincidental indicators* measure how the economy is doing right now. The gross national product (GNP) is the best-known example of a coincidental economic indicator.

Leading economic indicators are ones that tend to move ahead of the GNP and the other coincidental indicators. They tend to forecast what the economy is about to become. Economists have found 12 of these leading measures. Housing starts are one; orders for durable goods (heavy machinery) are another. History shows that an increase in these measures tends to foreshadow a better GNP.

One of the 12 leading indicators turned out to be the S&P 500 stock index. Economists had determined, after poring over a hundred years of data, that stock prices tended to predict the future condition of the economy. This is important since it should allow us to eliminate all economic data that is classified as coincidental or lagging in the quest to predict stock prices.

Theoretically, this left 11 leading indicators that might be useful to predict stock prices. Although the 12 leading indicators were all in the same time category, maybe one of the 12 was slightly more leading and so might signal, just marginally, the direction of stock prices. If so, one might be able to use this economic indicator to consistently predict what the market was about to do. So I took 40 years of data and overlaid each of the 11 leading indicators on top of the chart for stock prices. I discovered that, except for these two others, the stock market seemed to be one of the most leading of the 12 indicators.

In summary, I could only find three economic time series that were useful at times for forecasting stock prices: housing starts, money supply, and short-term interest rates, with the best correlation being with interest rates. The first two were leading economic indicators, but interest rates, oddly enough, were a lagging indicator, therefore presenting a major paradox. The act of using interest rates to predict stock prices is the illogical act of using a lagging indicator to forecast a leading one. However illogical this was, the charts didn't lie—the correlation was there. Resolving this paradox became an important milestone.

Earnings Didn't Seem to Work

During this time I also performed an interesting test regarding the use of earnings to predict stock prices. I did it in front of a small audience of around 10 people. First I showed them a graph of the earnings of the S&P 500 over a random 40-year period, without identifying the time period. I then asked these people to indicate where they would want to buy the S&P 500 and where they would want to sell it, using only this foreknowledge of earnings. After studying the earnings chart, the group finally agreed on where they would buy and sell. Then I brought out the chart of the S&P 500 and overlaid it against the earnings chart and their decisions.

The result was eye-opening. There were times when the foreknowledge of the earnings caused them to buy near a major price low and sell near a major price high, which was good, but just as often it didn't. There was one 5-year period of tremendous earnings growth, where stock prices actually declined, and their timing of the S&P 500 purchase was completely wrong. From this, I came to the conclusion that timing the market based on earnings data was very difficult at best. There were too many times when stock prices would move for years opposite to what the earnings seemed to indicate they should. That is too long a period to be wrong with one's investments; at least it is for me.

I am not of the temperament to hold a bearish position, then watch prices rise 20% for 3 months. Unless an indicator (technical or fundamental) correlates closely with market tops and bottoms, I don't find it useful. How close is close? It has to be pretty close; in other words, if a viewpoint about the market is correct, within a short time frame, you must see prices actually move in the direction of that viewpoint. When they don't, then the viewpoint must be doubted. You must apply this guideline, however, with a tremendous amount of wisdom. In fact, knowing exactly how long to hold a bullish or bearish view that goes against what stock prices are doing is the true art and skill of investing.

This simple study, showing very loose correlation between corporate earnings and the direction of the stock market, disabused me of any idea that forecasting earnings could help me make correct decisions about the direction of stock prices. However, this idea is widely believed by the vast majority of investors and analysts. Therefore, I want to be very careful in explaining what I mean because from another perspective it is possible to see that earnings do determine stock prices—at least over the long term.

All you have to do is take any long-term Securities Research chartbook and look for all the companies whose prices have been in growth patterns longer than 10 years. You will find in every case that these stocks also have long-term growth patterns for their earnings. There is no doubt that earnings do matter, but on closer inspection the same long-term charts also show periods lasting 6 to 9 months where prices went opposite to this long-term trend, and sometimes these countermoves were severe percentagewise.

Although earnings do matter over the very long term, they are not a good tool for trying to predict the tops or bottoms of major market moves.

Technical Analysis Did Seem to Work

As I said earlier, I could only find three economic-type indicators that, when overlaid on stock prices, would have allowed a person, at times, to predict the beginning of significant market ups and downs. Certain technical indicators, however, provided a much better correlation to these movements.

Technical analysis often incites a certain type of criticism. The criticism is usually based on the idea that stock prices must reflect some real economic value, and since technical analysis measures data that are not economic, it can't be measuring the really important information. For example, how can a shrinking number of stocks making new highs signal an imminent market decline? What does that have to do with earnings or the economic picture? Don't markets advance or decline for economic reasons?

It never bothered me that an indicator had nothing to do with economics. As long as it correlated with tops or bottoms is all that matters. For example, I found, after detailed tests, that the very best indicator of major market tops or bottoms comes from data that measure investor expectation. In my experience, extremes in investor sentiment correlate with major market tops and bottoms better than any other measure. This fact eventually forces any student of the market to elevate the theory of contrary opinion to the highest order and then confront and resolve any inconsistencies this creates.

THE MARKET THAT LIES AHEAD

This book is a summary of the knowledge I've gained over the past 30 years, applied to the stock market in 2002. In 1972, I promised myself that I would write a book the next time the market showed the classic signs of a major top. I had read that all great bull markets always end with the public speculating wildly in the stock market after a long bull run, with talk of much higher prices to come. That promise was realized with the publication of my first book, *A Strategic Guide to the Coming Roller Coaster Market*, in July 2000. Now that the thesis of that book appears to have materialized, it is important to focus closely on the different swings that will make up this new period. It is my belief that we are again entering the type of market we had in the 1970s, except that this time it will be much shorter (5 to 7 years), and it will occur for entirely different reasons.

The reason will have to be financial in nature. You will see in Chapter 3 that two numbers go into the equations to determine stock prices: dividends (earnings) and interest rates. The equations are in the form of fractions. The long trading range in the 1970s was created by the opposing action of two powerful forces: Ever-increasing earnings (primarily due to inflation) were being neutralized in the fractions by higher interest rates. In a fraction, if you double both the numerator and denominator, you end up with the same result. These two forces were almost perfectly in balance during the 1970s, resulting in the long trading range of the 1970s.

However, this time I think the opposite will occur: The negative effect of lower growth for earnings and dividends in the fractions will be mathematically offset by declining interest rates. Here, the numerator and denominator will both reduce, resulting in the same value 5 years from now as we have today.

THE FOUR INVESTING PARADOXES

A few strange and important paradoxes confront the investor, and these must ultimately be resolved before you can understand the stock market completely.

I will state them here, but must read the ensuing chapters to find their resolution. Although the paradoxes seem simple, they are not; they contain some great truths about investing. You could read a whole book explaining the stock market but you still be confused about investing simply because these four paradoxes are not given the focus they truly deserve. Resolving them is fundamental to any basic investment understanding.

Paradox 1: I'm Happy When I'm Sad.

In September 1997, the government announced good economic news: Payroll levels were increasing. The market fell 100 points. The press was in a quandary to explain it. Analysts said that good news often means that the Federal Reserve will raise rates, and this is not good. If this is true, however, then carried to its extreme, the better the economy gets, the more the market should sell off. When is good news really bad and bad news really good?

Paradox 2: How Can the Tail Wag the Dog?

The stock market is one of 12 leading economic indicators, probably the best of the 12. To predict the stock market, people usually turn to interest rates. Here is the paradox: The U.S. government classifies interest rates as a lagging economic indicator. It is one of the last things to move in a business cycle. Why do people use a lagging economic indicator to determine what a leading indicator is about to do? How can the tail wag the dog?

Paradox 3: The Technician Says Up and the Fundamentalist Says Down, yet Both Are Right.

Trying to determine the direction of stock prices, the fundamental analyst looks at the economic situation, proclaims that all is well, and says that stocks will advance. The technician, after studying new highs and lows, the advance-decline line, and price patterns, says that the stock market will decline. Both are right. How can this be?

Paradox 4: One Million Investors Are Usually Wrong.

In the stock market, when everyone says the market will advance, it generally starts to decline. When everyone thinks the market is in or starting into a bear market, it is usually after the fact, and the market is now ready to rise. What is the true reason that the market behaves in such a contradictory fashion, and what does it mean?

1

Trading Price Swings

A NEW MARKET PARADIGM

At a series of client seminars in February 2000, I made the following statement.

> As we begin the millennium, this 18-year bull market shows all the technical, fundamental, and speculative signs of completion. I am not saying that we are entering a bear market, which when ended, will then allow the resumption of the current bull market. I am saying that we have been in the topping process that will lead into a larger-scale correction. I do not believe we are facing a market crash. I think we're facing a time correction, an extended sideways up-and-down movement that encompasses a number of bull and bear markets.

My thesis was that the 18-year bull market, which began in 1982, with the Dow Jones industrials just under 800, was displaying the classic signs of a major market top. You would think that the classic signs of a major price top are certain economic conditions, but they aren't. The classic signs are (and have always been):

- Extreme overspeculation and interest in stock investing by the public (higher this time than during previous major market tops)
- Very high levels of bullish sentiment, comparable to previous major tops in many indicators

- Large technical divergences in the major market indices (a fact that was being rationalized away by many market technicians who wanted to remain bullish)
- Broad talk of a new era, in which the old rules about stock values no longer apply

In forecasting the end of the 18-year bull market, the problem wasn't so much seeing these classic signs or even deciding they were of sufficient volume to imply a major top. The key was truly believing that these signs were more important than the economic reasons being offered for why prices would go much higher. Once this was accepted, the real difficulty was trying to predict the time, magnitude, and form of the ensuing correction.

I believe a large percentage of investors were expecting some sort of correction, but I think the common belief was that, once the correction was over, the old bull market would resume. I disagreed with that. Bull markets that reach a level of speculative excess like this one are not normally corrected with one declining wave. Therefore, a lengthy trading range market seemed the most probable and was the one postulated. Now that the first declining wave of the correction is no longer just an idea, we are in a much better position to forecast the possible structure and form the complete correction will take.

A Trading Range Market

The ending of a long bull market always brings new experiences for younger investors. Younger investors couldn't remember a time when stock prices didn't go up. During long bull markets, investing becomes too easy—you put your money in, do nothing, and the market takes care of everything. Investors come to think that these spectacular and easy gains are normal and forget that other types of stock markets ever existed. However, the last 20 years have been abnormal times, and it is a mistake to think they are normal. A famous quote from market lore warns against this mindset of high-level normalcy: "Never mistake brains for a bull market."

It is also a mistake to think that all booms will be followed by busts, that periods of extreme overspeculation are always followed by crashes. More often than not, the excess valuations driven into prices by a euphoric public are slowly dissipated by prices going up and down, making little forward progress for some time.

> Stock prices don't go straight up or straight down; they move in jerks and starts. For example, a price advance lasting 4 weeks may go strong for 3 days and then hold for 5 days before moving higher again. These brief holding periods act like mini-corrections, effectively slowing the advance to a more normal rate.
>
> The same can happen on a much larger scale, forming what is called a *trading range*. A ***trading range market*** is a period in which stock prices go up and down repeatedly, essentially moving sideways. Prices stay within a price band, with the trading range defined by the highs and lows.

Investors must be reminded that there have been many times in the past when prices didn't go up but trended in long sideways trading ranges. In fact, three major trading range markets have occurred in the past hundred years. During these times, the natural return from stocks falls off dramatically. The first long trading range was the 15 years between 1906 and 1920. The Dow started 1906 at a price of 75 and, after going back and forth in a number of bull and bear markets, finished the year 1920 at a price of 64. Then there was the 12-year period between 1937 and 1949, when the Dow was at 195 in March 1937, ending at a price of 160 by June 1949.

The most recent trading range period was the 16 years between 1966 and 1982. In 1966, the Dow first hit the 1,000 mark. During the following 16 years, it traded between 700 and 1,000 a number of times, making little progress. It wasn't until late 1982 that it finally broke through 1,000 for good. Figure 1.1 shows this most recent period using the Standard & Poor (S&P) 500 index. During these periods, trading market swings again become a popular investment strategy.

Market Timing versus Buy and Hold

It may seem strange to hear that trading market swings was ever an accepted investment strategy. After all, who hasn't heard that investors should not try to time the market or the advice, "It isn't *timing the market* that's important but *time in the market*"? The buy-and-hold investment philosophy is very well entrenched. Its success over the last 10 years of continuously rising prices is unquestioned. However, this philosophy has been espoused primarily by the mutual fund industry, which

FIGURE 1.1 This chart, published in July 2000 before the market decline, shows my expectation of the start of a new trading range market. The straight line at the bottom shows the stock market's trendline since 1928. Notice how the 1982–2000 bull market took prices far away from this trendline. It is normal to expect a trading range that works prices back closer to the line.

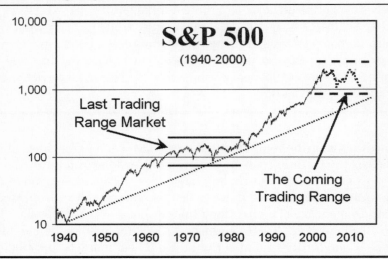

wants your money to stay put. The other philosophy—market timing—has been popular during periods when market conditions required it. Let me clarify these two competing theories on how investors should approach stock market investing: buy and hold and market timing.

Buy and hold is the philosophy that you should buy a large basket of good stocks and hold them over long periods, ignoring the intervening price swings. Investors who practice buy and hold believe that predicting price movements is either too difficult or too costly. They recognize that stock price increases through all the bull and bear markets, including the Great Crash of 1929 to 1932, have averaged more than 10% per year. Therefore, if you just hold onto your investments and ignore the wiggles, you will emerge just fine.

Market timing, on the other hand, is the philosophy that you will do better if you try to catch the upswings and sell just before the major downswings. Investors who practice market timing think that it can be done in an advantageous and profitable way. They believe that strategies that attempt to time the market are more natural than buy and hold and that such strategies follow the normal tendencies of investors to avoid losing principal.

Which investment philosophy is better? This question is really answered by determining the type of market one is in. I don't think there is any doubt that, in long bull markets, the buy-and-hold philosophy does best. Like many others, I've seen that almost any effort to time price movements during a long bull market generally worsens the investment return, sometimes considerably.

Over long trading range markets, however, buy and hold does not work well. Almost any well-thought-out trading strategy does better than the simple buy and hold. The question of which is the better strategy becomes the question of determining what type of stock market one expects to have in the near future.

Since I believe that we have entered a trading range market, I think that investors are going to be very disappointed with the investment results they get from the buy-and-hold strategy. Investors will have to learn to trade the swings of the market, just like their forebears did during other trading range periods. To be successful, they will have to gain a lot more investment knowledge and skill—much more than the do-nothing approach required of the buy-and-hold method.

Isn't Everyone Really a Market Timer?

I claim that even investors who have been invested for a long time are in fact market timers. There is always a day when they buy stocks and a day when they sell them. It seems that most people consider it okay to market time as long as one is timing the long-term trend and the basis of the decision is some fundamental value formula. But that is semantics—it is still market timing. For example, it is considered acceptable if you decided to buy stocks in 1980, when price and earnings (PE) ratios were 10, and decided to sell them in 1999, when the PE ratios got to 35. Although this is market timing, it seems to be considered acceptable market timing. The question then is, "How long do you have to hold an investment before it crosses the line from market timing to buy and hold?" There is no realistic answer, so the idea of market timing is really that of degrees.

The buy-and-hold philosophy says, "Don't sell every time the news gets bad and the market begins a severe decline." In other words, don't react to quick price changes. However, how do you avoid major crashes that wipe people out or what *do* you do when the stock market has entered a long trading range? Investors will become very disappointed with buy and hold as they watch their investments fall, rise, and then fall again and again. Their investment returns will come off the previous higher

levels, and they'll notice that doing nothing, which worked so well before, is no longer working. They'll become willing to consider the idea
that it might be okay to sell their stocks after a 30% gain and be out of the
market, waiting on the sidelines for a new opportunity to present itself.
During a trading range market, the price action slowly induces people to
become market timers.

Why Buy and Hold Is Hard to Apply

Although theoretically sound and well intentioned, the buy-and-hold
strategy is very difficult for investors to apply. Why? It is a little like
telling someone that the way to walk from Los Angeles to New York is
simply to put one foot in front of the other until you arrive. You can't
argue with the instructions, but can anyone really do it? The formula
omits too many important details.

The basic concept behind buy and hold is the idea that when investors try to time the market, more often than not, they buy at the top
and sell at the bottom. Moreover, many studies on market timing have
shown that when you factor in timing errors and commissions, investors
would be better off leaving their investments alone. I do not argue
against these conclusions here (but I will in Chapter 8); in fact, I will
agree with them. After accepting these arguments, however, I still believe market timing is preferable—even if it produces a worse result on
paper. How can I say that? With market timing, there is a better chance
that the investor will be around to earn that smaller return than if he or
she tries to buy and hold because the buy-and-hold philosophy omits a
fundamental factor from the equation.

Buy and hold is predicated on the belief that the investor will never
have a strong opinion about the direction of stock prices, or if the investor does have a strong opinion, will refrain from acting on it. Right
there is the problem. More often than not the first part is true; an investor does not have a strong opinion and so is willing to wait and see
what happens. At other times, however, the investor will develop a very
strong opinion. He or she becomes sure of what is going to happen next
and, whether right or wrong, acts on this certainty. Let me illustrate with
an example of a possible conversation between and advisor an his client.

CLIENT: My stocks have gone down 10% and things aren't looking
   very good.

ADVISOR: Yes, I know, but just stay put and all will be okay.

Two weeks later:

> CLIENT: My account is now down 15%. The market fell almost every day over the last 2 weeks. The newspeople are saying that the economy is going to get worse and the future looks pretty bad. There isn't any reason for stocks to go up.
>
> ADVISOR: Yes, but don't do anything—we planned to buy and hold.

One week later, with the stock market selling off severely:

> CLIENT: Sell me out before I lose any more money.
>
> ADVISOR: I hear you, but remember we intended to buy and hold.
>
> CLIENT: That's what you've said for the last 3 weeks, and it has cost me a lot of money. Now I'm sure the market is going lower, absolutely sure. There isn't one good reason for it to go up. Are you telling me that I should voluntarily stand pat and lose more money? Let's at least get out and, once prices move lower, we can get back in. Do what I tell you or I'll get a new advisor who can see what's happening.

When investors reach a point of certainty or conviction, they act on that certainty. To ask them to do otherwise—to refrain from action at those moments—is like asking them not to turn the steering wheel to avoid the train they see coming right at them, whether that train is real or not.

Therefore, it is my belief that market timing is a more natural investment strategy to use than the buy-and-hold method. As an added benefit, once investors are willing to consider market timing and give it a try, they now have the luxury of thoroughly planning what kind of timing strategy to use. This advance planning should help investors sidestep market timing based on emotional decisions that truly do destroy investor confidence and investment returns.

As mentioned, market timing is much more difficult to execute than the do-nothing approach of buy and hold. To do market timing, you have to establish an opinion about what is going to happen in the market. You need a basis to believe that the market is now ready to go up or go down. You also have to know that there are times when no opinion is possible, the market is unpredictable, and no forecast should be made. To do these things you have to know when and how to develop an investment opinion.

DEVELOPING AN INVESTMENT OPINION

Stock market investing, or speculation, is one of the most exciting activities you can undertake. The word *speculation* comes from the Latin word *speculare*, which means "to look." The problem is that there are simply too many things to look at. Stacked top to bottom, one page at a time, Wall Street probably produces over 20 feet of data on any given trading day. Lack of data is not the problem—in fact, the problem is the opposite: the overwhelming volume of data and not knowing what is important and what isn't. Without realizing that more than 99% of the data on Wall Street are immaterial to an investment decision, most people simply get lost in the confusion of too much information.

Most investors think that to make timely, correct investment decisions, you must pore over this mountain of data and know many facts. I have found that the opposite is true. You achieve insight by simplifying your thinking, by focusing on only a few important points and never deviating from those points. You do this by continually discarding the mountain of unnecessary information to find the few important concepts.

Early in my studies, I had a friend who used more than 100 indicators to analyze the stock market. At first, I envied his superior knowledge, but eventually I came to feel sorry for him: He was always confused. I finally figured out that he simply had too much information. At any given time, only one or two points were vital, and the rest just served to divert his attention to unimportant and contradictory data. He had never learned that the secret to a clear and accurate picture of the market is finding the few truly important pieces of information and downplaying or discarding everything else.

Holding to an Investment Viewpoint or Position

Holding to an investment viewpoint or opinion is very similar to the action of anchoring yourself at a location against a physical force. If you are facing a strong wind, you have to anchor your feet in firm ground or get blown away. Similarly, when you hold a market viewpoint, that viewpoint must be anchored in facts and theories that you know are correct and true. You must solidly believe them, and they must be founded on established and tested ideas. Otherwise, you will not be able to hold to your investment position, and your viewpoint will flip-flop in the face of almost any concept or compelling idea that comes along.

I remember the first time I saw this happen in myself. It was embarrassing how flimsy my ideas proved to be and how vulnerable they were to contradictory evidence. Although much of my wavering was attributable to age and inexperience, I wasn't used to seeing it in myself. I stood there amazed as I watched my opinions flip-flop like a rag doll throughout the day.

That time was October 1971, after Nixon had announced wage and price controls. I had just become interested in the stock market and was working at night, watching the stock market every day on the new stock market channel, KWHY, in the Los Angeles area. I was learning by reading books and listening to brokers, commentators, and economists discuss the economy and the market.

Prices had rallied for 2 weeks after Nixon's announcement, and I became, like everyone else, bullish. Then, the market started a mild-sell off that soon stopped. I expected prices to begin a major rally and so bought two stocks—my first trades in fact. In a few days, the market started to decline again, and then the selling really started to pick up steam. It declined almost every day, and I started to get nervous.

I began listening in earnest to every commentator, trying to understand what was happening. On one particular day, I got bullish, bearish, then bullish again, agreeing each time with the bullish or bearish arguments of each commentator who came on the air. My ideas were like papier-mâché against almost any idea.

I wasn't used to this. I had studied mathematics and the physical sciences, and in these disciplines there is always one clear answer. Now, I was unable to hold to my ideas against almost any other idea that was expressed. It was obvious to me that I didn't know anything. If I was to become successful, I would have to establish for myself what was important and what wasn't. Only then would I be able to say, "That's balderdash," or "That is important." It would take a lot of study, experience, practice, and application.

Finding Out What Is Important

Countless books have been written on technical analysis. The majority of market technicians have read them all, and yet history usually finds them holding wrong opinions at critical market junctures. The problem isn't with the information in these books—the basic data and theories are correct. The problem is that the books often omit the practical instruction on how to apply the information in real time. For example, when two important indicators are pointing to opposite scenarios for the market, how do you determine which one to choose?

Stock market books seldom address this question, but it is key to the whole activity. I'll tell you the answer: To achieve understanding, you must find out what is truly important, rank the data by relative importance, and then learn how to fit the rankings together to see the correct stock market story. Yes, stock markets do tell stories through their price action. The art is learning how to use the available statistical information to figure out the story. The friend I mentioned previously failed because the books never instructed him on how to put all 100 indicators together to see what that story is. He became immersed in all the indicators, looking for some great truth. He missed the idea that these were only clues to help uncover the story the stock market was telling.

Evaluating the relative importance of data is extremely important. Much of the information that Wall Street uses to think with is simply wrong or not really vital. Without correct information or information that is correctly evaluated, you can't reach correct conclusions. Moreover, sometimes because of excessive publicity, it is very difficult to evaluate a fact: The data have been made to appear more important—or less important—than they are. This distortion, too, can make it difficult to reach correct conclusions.

Following are two examples. The first concerns the current popular idea about the strength of the baby boomer wave. The second concerns the question of whether stock prices are controlled by an invisible set of insiders.

The Baby Boomer Misconception

Whenever I see an idea that has wide acceptance in the investment community, I start looking for the holes in it. I do this because of my deep belief in the theory of contrary opinion (explained in Chapter 5). When I saw Wall Street fall in love with the idea that the baby boomer wave would drive stock prices higher for another 8 years, I got very interested. At a seminar where a hundred brokers were listening to this idea, I saw almost every head nodding in agreement. So I did my own study of the situation.

The baby boomer idea is a simple one. It holds that money drives the stock market and that the expanding number of baby boomers reaching their prime investment and buying years (ages 45 to 48) is a huge, irresistible force that will drive stock prices higher for a long time. Figure 1.2 shows the correlation between stock prices and the number of people turning 45. The idea is that age 45 is generally the point at which a person has the greatest purchasing power. This buying is good for business and translates to higher prices for stocks. Forty-five is also the age when the average person starts saving and investing the maximum amount, as they approach retirement. The way the stock market seems to follow the population curve is uncanny. The chart leads people to these conclusions:

- The baby boomer wave is very large.
- There is a strong correlation between stock prices and the number of people turning 45.
- The stock market will continue to rise until the year 2007.

This chart makes a strong visual impact and can create unswerving conviction about the power of the baby boomer wave. Both the plausibility of the idea and the strong correlation between the two curves give the baby boomer idea its wide acceptance and apparent importance.

FIGURE 1.2 The popular baby boomer wave graph, which shows the number of people turning 45 plotted against the inflation-adjusted S&P 500.

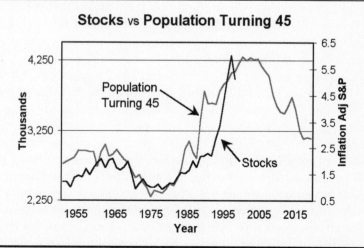

Notice that the baby boomer idea does not consider the possibility that stock prices may already be too high. The concept is simple: With a large number of people turning 45, stock prices will continue to rise due to their sheer buying power.

When I started studying the baby boomer data, the first thing I noticed was that the Y-axis started not at zero but at 2.25 million births. This had the effect of making the births after WWII look larger than they really are. More importantly, I concluded that the chart plotted the wrong item. The more important and accurate item to plot is the *percentage* of the population turning 45, not the actual number. Certainly, 1 million people turning 45 when the population is 300 million ($\frac{1}{3}\%$) is less important than 1 million people turning 45 in a population of 100 million (1%). As the population gets larger, a larger number of people are needed to produce a comparable economic impact. I calculated the percentage of the population turning 45 and graphed that against the same inflation-adjusted S&P 500.

Figure 1.3, plotting the percentage of the population turning 45 against the stock market, presents an entirely different picture:

- The baby boomer wave exists, but it's much smaller and less important than many people think.
- The wave might be peaking right now.

Therefore, the idea of the stock market constantly advancing against a wave of baby boomers is far overrated. If the stock market is too high and the economy is facing real economic problems, prices can and will decline—and decline severely. In fact, this baby boomer idea has all the classic signs of an old pattern: Near the top of a major bull market, a new idea emerges that convinces people that a new era has arrived and that bear markets are a thing of the past.

Stock market lore holds that every great bull market generates such ideas. (Because of it, well-schooled investors usually greet the emergence of a new era as one of the classic signs of a bull market end.) The new era always signifies a new viewpoint and originates from the unique ideas and apparent new economy of each period. The new era appears so powerful and so obviously right that a bear market seems almost impossible. Investors usually ignore any negative ideas because they seem so unimportant when viewed against the new economic viewpoint and because they think any correction will be relatively mild. As soon as a correction continues and slips into a major bear market, people's thoughts about stocks shift, and the fallacy in the idea is soon uncovered.

FIGURE 1.3   The percentage of the population turning 45 plotted against an inflation-adjusted S&P 500. This chart shows that the baby boomer wave is not as important as some have said.

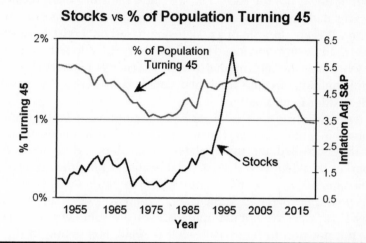

Do Insiders Control the Market?

One of the most persuasive—and pervasive—of the old ideas is the theory that stock prices are controlled and manipulated by a large and powerful group of insiders. Over the years, I've investigated this idea in its many guises—from corporate insiders, to mutual fund money managers, to stock exchange specialists—and I have always found it to be false.

My first contact with this idea came in 1971, when it was popular to assume that the specialists on the floor of the exchange control stock prices. All orders to buy and sell are processed through a specialist, who matches and executes all incoming buy and sell orders for a stock. The specialist also has the famous black book. This book (now a computer) contains all the orders made away from the market that clients have entered with their brokers—orders to buy or sell if the stock hits a certain price. With these data, the specialist knows at what price heavy demand and heavy supply will occur.

Besides matching up orders, specialists are also charged with buying and selling in their own accounts to help stabilize prices if supply and demand get out of balance. Because specialists trading for their own accounts can amount to approximately 20% of the daily trading volume, this is significant. The black book and insider trading led to the belief that specialists control stock prices to their advantage. At one time, a specialist short-selling indicator seemed to prove this contention. However, by 1974, after a careful analysis of specialist data, I was able to prove to myself that this is not the case. The specialist data and the indicator that technicians had invented were not measuring what technicians thought they were. It is an example of a conclusion based on a mistaken concept. Therefore, I became convinced that floor specialists do not control price movements over the intermediate or long term. As I analyzed more and more information, I came to similar conclusions about other forms of possible insider manipulation.

It was once true that markets were manipulated and conspiracies were possible, but no longer. Furthermore, holding to the viewpoint that prices are controlled and manipulated by insiders is destructive to correct market thinking. It is destructive because *it puts the cause of stock price movements, and therefore your ability to predict these movements, outside your perimeter of knowledge.* When you discover, by careful analysis, that prices are not manipulated, you are somewhat free; you are finally in a position to figure out what is really happening in the stock market.

Daniel Drew, Robber Baron

Daniel Drew was the king of stock manipulation and short selling— one of the infamous robber barons of 200 years ago. His story illustrates how it used to be.

Daniel Drew was born in New England around 1800. A man of low business ethics, he prided himself on the swindle. One idea he invented was that of *watering the stock.* As a young cattle drover, he would deliver a large herd and then have his men lay out salt for the cows to lick. The next morning he allowed the thirsty cows to drink until they almost burst. The butchers, faced with the fattest cows they had ever seen, paid top dollar.

Later, Drew gained control of the Erie Railroad and became rich by manipulating Erie stock. He would sell the stock short and then release bad news about the company. After the price fell, he would profit by buying back the shares at the low price. He would then release good news. He did this repeatedly until, after 10 years, the Erie was almost bankrupt and Drew was a rich man.

He also participated in one of the most colorful financial battles in American history. Commodore Vanderbilt got tired of the Scandal of the Erie and decided to buy the company away from Drew by secretly purchasing a majority of shares on the New York Stock Exchange. Drew, with the help of Jim Fisk and Jay Gould, fought back. Using the company printing press, the three printed illegal shares of Erie, flooding the exchange with counterfeit stock as Vanderbilt's brokers purchased every share in sight. On learning that he held worthless stock, Vanderbilt sent the law after the trio, who now had his money. The three went to New Jersey, bribed state officials, and fended off the Vanderbilt legal attack. Eventually, they returned Vanderbilt's money and he abandoned his efforts to buy the Erie.

A while later, Drew, having again shorted Erie stock, was caught in one of his own traps. Jay Gould, Drew's former sidekick, wiped him out by manipulating the price higher, thereby forcing Drew to buy back stock at astronomically high prices.

The era of the robber barons is long gone now, and the use of inside information and the release of misleading data to manipulate stock prices are now illegal. There is no longer a powerful *they* who can control stock prices. We don't know how investors survived in an environment like that, but somehow they did, long enough to bring about the reforms that created the fairer markets we enjoy today. (Source: Kean Collection/ Archive Photos™.)

WHAT'S COMING NEXT?

Market timing presents the purist with a major theoretical problem. The standard academic models for stock prices hold that stock prices are basically random and unpredictable. If I and many others believe that market timing is possible, we must have a different model in mind than these academic models. Chapter 2 introduces the stock market model that I use to understand price movements. It allows for a stock market that is sometimes predictable and therefore makes market timing possible.

The model provides further benefit in its ability to align and unify other stock market information that was previously confusing or in conflict. For example, for years an argument has raged between the market technician and the market fundamentalist about whose discipline is better at predicting the stock market. As you will eventually see, both disciplines are correct when applied to the correct time scale.

During a long bull market, when the buy-and-hold philosophy works so well, it is not so important to clarify these points. During a trading range market, it is vital. To time the market successfully, you must establish two points: (1) the expected size and time scale of the price moves you want to catch and (2) methods to determine when the market has shifted from a random state into a predictable one. This requires skill and experience and—most importantly—a willingness to change your mind when you are wrong. You must learn how to do this in such a way that your confidence in your own judgment is not undermined.

What follows in this book is my understanding of what it will take to be successful through a market environment like this. I address the investment tools that I have come to use during 30 years of market study. If you are going to be successful through a market like the one I'm expecting, you will have to use many tools.

The following chapters explain how I use information to do this. In Chapter 3, you learn the role of the fair-value term *D/I* in this model. Chapters 4 and 5 explore the area of technical analysis, as well as why it can help locate unstable markets that are ready to undergo a strong feedback-loop movement. In Chapter 6, you'll see how new discoveries in chaos theory help explain the fractal nature of stock price charts and how they give a firmer theoretical foundation for the controversial Elliott wave theory.

Chapter 7 broadly outlines the pattern the market may make during its expected long sideways run. Chapter 8 presents certain studies I did a few years ago on strategies for sideways markets. These studies backtest various moving-average methods and how they performed on paper through the last trading range market, from 1966 to 1982. Alternative investments, such as hedge funds, are also discussed.

2

A New Stock
Market Model

SOLVING THE BIG THEORETICAL PROBLEM

Standard academic models for the stock market hold that stock prices are essentially random and unpredictable. Because of this, whenever people set about predicting the stock market, they are essentially disagreeing with these accepted models. Not having an answer, most analysts and commentators just keep writing their predictions, silently ignoring the paradox. Even if one accepts that these standard models are inaccurate and prices are sometimes predictable (as I do), there is another problem.

The investing public and Wall Street employees demand that analysts always have an opinion about the stock market. Even if an analyst believes that the market is predictable only at certain points, he or she is forced to express an opinion all the time to satisfy this need, knowing full well it is impossible to do. If analysts spoke only when they saw a very predictable market and refused to speak when they thought it was random, there would be more success.

There are many great technicians and market analysts who are skilled enough to accurately locate the beginning and end of the major price moves, with only a few false starts. I know this because I've seen them do it for the past 30 years.

In this chapter, with the help of a few ideas from chaos theory, I introduce the model I have come to use for the stock market. I believe this model is more accurate than the efficient market model, is closer to the beliefs of most traders, and allows for a sometimes predictable market. If this model is somewhat correct, one of the arts of investing is knowing when the market is predictable and when it is truly random.

The terms used in this model—fair value and feedback loops—have been expounded on by many other writers and used in other models. The form of the model that I present is, as far as I know, unique.

WHAT IS A MODEL?

What is a model? A *model* is either a mental construct or a physical system that is thought to behave in a similar way to the actual system under study. An effective model of the stock market would act parallel to the actual stock market, thereby allowing you to gain insight into what is happening.

The Old Model

Academicians generally use models developed from ideas tested in the 1960s and 1970s. One of the ideas postulated in these early models was that the market is highly efficient. An efficient market model says that the current price reflects everything that is known about a company and that large investors immediately react to any fresh economic news, adjusting prices to fair value almost instantaneously. Therefore, you can never get a leg up on the market. Any price deviation brought about by irrational investor activity is quickly brought back to fair value by the rationally informed. One conclusion from the efficient market model was that stock prices are fundamentally random and unpredictable, and therefore, you can't beat the market. Gordon Malkiel popularized this standard investment model in a book called *A Random Walk down Wall Street*.

A **model** is a mental construct or physical system that parallels or behaves like a real system. Studying the stock market model provides insight into and an understanding of how the stock market actually behaves.

What's Right with the Old Model

Although I never really agreed with the efficient market theory when I first read about it in 1971, I did agree with one concept that came out of it. The concept is that it is hard for an analyst or an investor to select a portfolio of a few individual stocks that will do better than a large index of stocks. What this means is that the portfolio that gives the best gains with the least risk is a portfolio of all stocks or an index of a large number of stocks. My immediate agreement came from my knowledge of an analogous problem in physics. Let me explain.

One subject that physicists study is the behavior of gases (e.g., oxygen, hydrogen). The starting assumption is that the gas consists of millions of free molecules, all moving very fast in short, straight lines until they bang into one another or against the walls of the container, ricocheting off in a new direction. To understand this situation, physicists don't attempt to apply Newton's equations of motion to each molecule and then add it all up to calculate the sum total. That is much too difficult. What they do is come at the problem statistically and figure out the average effect—the total effect of a bunch of them acting en masse. In other words, the behavior of a single molecule is unpredictable, but the behavior of a large number of them, acting together, is predictable.

Let me explain this in greater detail. Suppose a tiny molecule flies up against the wall of the container and bounces away, much as a billiard ball bounces off the rails of a pool table. This reversal in direction (momentum) of that tiny molecule causes a little kickback against the wall, just as the billiard ball kicks against the billiard table rail. It is impossible to calculate when any particular molecule is going to fly up against the wall and give it a little kick. However, we can calculate with some certainty that, in any given second, a certain number of molecules will probably hit the wall. The sum of all these little molecular kickbacks every second is the large-scale effect we experience as the pressure of the gas.

In physics, this theory of statistical mechanics states that although we can't know what any individual molecule is going to do, we can still know something about what a lot of molecules will do en masse. That behavior is predictable.

When I started my studies years ago, I assumed that this theory was probably true of the stock market and I asked the following question: If stock prices are predictable, does that predictability lie with being able to predict the performance of an individual stock or that of a bunch of stocks en masse (i.e., the stock market)? I guessed that if the stock market is predictable, that predictability would be found in forecasting the overall stock market, not an individual stock.

Therefore, this book presents no stock-picking methods. I believe you'll be more successful if you look for predictable periods in the overall trend of the market and then ride with it by buying an index of the market or a large diversified fund. If you can't be successful at that, you will probably not be successful at predicting the direction of individual stocks. The book is based on this assumption.

What's Wrong with the Old Model

People who made their living trading the market on a daily basis often disagreed with the traditional academic models. Most experienced traders had seen markets that were predictable or that sometimes seemed to be, so the efficient market model didn't match their experience. The traders found it very difficult to describe their experiences and perceptions to the academicians. The statistical mathematics used in academia often seemed to obscure the realities that traders had observed (statistical mathematics can often obscure subtle but important points).

One assumption in the efficient model is that any price disturbance away from fair value, created by emotional or irrational investor activity, is small and is quickly neutralized by the large rational investors. This seemed like a reasonable assumption. In fact, it was the same assumption that physicists and engineers had been making in their disciplines for years. They, too, had assumed that if you created a small disturbance in a physical system, that disturbance would quickly disappear, being dispersed or carried away by frictional forces or something. They couldn't prove this assumption since the mathematics were too difficult, but it seemed likely. All this changed in the in the 1970s and 1980s, as mathematicians and physicists made new discoveries. They slowly found that their assumption wasn't always true, and that given the right conditions, small disturbances can actually go the other way; at certain times they carry forward and magnify into very large disturbances.

The finance professors knew the efficient market model wasn't quite accurate, but they assumed that it was accurate enough to be a practical model. They made the same mistake that the physical scientists had made, assuming that small price disturbances that carried prices *away* from fair value would quickly *return* to fair value. Now this was in doubt. These discoveries confirmed what many traders had been trying to describe, that irrational price activity is often a much bigger effect than previously thought, and not so easily dismissed. Sometimes prices take on a life of their own and the irrational movements become much larger and more important than originally thought. Many of these basic discoveries in physics, mathematics, and finance were explained and eventually classified under the heading of chaos theory, which Gluck made popular in his excellent book, *Chaos*.

Adding a Little Chaos to the Model: The Feedback Loop

To understand how chaos enters the picture, we must take a closer look at something called a feedback loop. Feedback loops are a fundamental concept in various branches of chaos theory and are very important here, too.

By the way, the theory of chaos doesn't hold that everything is chaotic, as the name might imply. Chaos theory slowly emerged when scientists in a number of unrelated fields started finding hidden order in a variety of systems originally thought to be chaotic. Scientists soon recognized that concepts such as exact order and total chaos were absolute conditions never really found in nature, and that real physical systems existed somewhere between the extremes. At times, systems with a lot of chaotic motion naturally dampen down and become orderly, whereas orderly systems, when slightly disturbed, often become very chaotic. Chaos theory arose as a way to define something that comprises both order and chaos and that provides ways to determine when a model can ignore one or the other. A key concept behind this type of behavior is called a feedback loop.

Because feedback loops are so important in understanding my new model and because the best way to explain a feedback loop is to give you a few examples of it, let's look at two very common ones. The first is probably the clearest and simplest example. The second is a physical situation, with feedback loops very similar to those found in the stock market.

You'll certainly recognize the first example (Figure 2.1). When listening to a lecture that uses an amplification system, have you ever heard that screeching sound when the volume is too high? Everything is going along fine, and then a terrible loud noise overwhelms the audience. This is a feedback loop in action. Sound enters the microphone, goes to the amplifier, and comes out of the speakers at a higher volume. This amplified sound, besides entering the listeners' ears, also reenters the microphone. If the volume knob is set high enough, the amplitude of the

FIGURE 2.1   A common feedback loop—the screeching sound system.

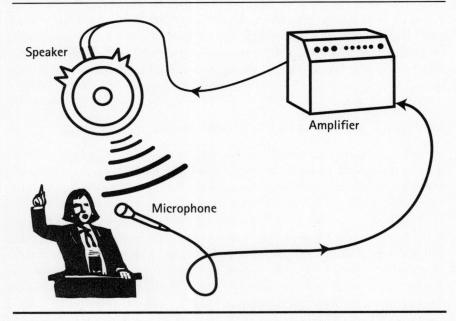

sound reentering the microphone is higher than the original sound. This cycle repeats, the sound building and building, until you hear that terrible screech. Even if the lecturer stops talking, the sound continues. The lecturer initiates the sound, but once the feedback starts, it continues and builds on its own, feeding on itself. When you understand the concept, you can find many examples of feedback loops in nature. One that is very similar to the feedback loops found in the stock market is the physical situation of an avalanche.

The pre-avalanche condition starts with a large blanket of snow on the side of a mountain. The blanket grows as more and more snow falls, yet nothing happens. Although you can't see it from the surface, weather

---

A ***feedback loop*** is an energy system that occurs naturally or by design in which some of the energy or disturbance produced comes back, adding to the system's ability to create or direct more energy. A feedback loop is a self-amplifying effect.

and the pressure of the accumulating snow is causing the crystalline structure of the snow to become unstable. All that is needed is a triggering event. One day, a small bird lands at the top of the snow bank and breaks a little piece free, which triggers the underlying instability. The small piece of snow falls and loosens a larger chunk below it. This chunk falls on the snow below it, breaking even more snow free. Finally, an entire hillside of snow cascades and falls to the base of the mountain (Figure 2.2). After the avalanche has occurred, the hillside is stable. Although a bird could trigger an avalanche when the snow bank is unstable, 20

FIGURE 2.2   The avalanche is a feedback system very similar to the type found in the stock market. Once a major instability has been triggered, it can feed and build on itself.

stomping elephants couldn't start one when the snow is stable. It will not collapse until enough new snow has fallen on the hillside to make it unstable again.

The important concept to understand here is that *the cause of the avalanche is the avalanche itself.* In all feedback loops, the rapidly repeated movement that creates the ongoing effect is caused by the structure of the system, not by the triggering event. Although a bird triggered the first movement, its continuation depends on the instability of the snow bank. This is also true of the audio feedback in the first example: The screech continues even after the speaker stops talking. A small beginning effect is magnified into a large one by the structure of the system; this is one of the main discoveries that has come out of the new science of chaos. The phenomenon is often colorfully described in chaos theory by the phrase "how the flapping of the wings of a butterfly in San Rafael can give rise to a hurricane over Texas."

The stock market, too, has feedback loops. A single news item may trigger the initial selling, but then selling begets more selling, and the movement takes on a life of its own. Here, however, the source of the underlying instability can be complex. For now, I will say that its source seems to lie in the group emotions of investors and the magnitude and distribution of investors' profits or losses.

Older stock market models downplayed these feedback loops. They held that these types of price distortions are quickly erased by large, rational investors, who neutralize them by bringing prices back to fair value. However, it was chaos theory that demonstrated that these types of distortions can be much more powerful than previously thought and therefore not so easily dismissed.

My work indicates that feedback loops alone seem to be able to cause price movements of up to 25% or more. This is an important conclusion and I want to state it clearly: The stock market can become unstable at times and undergo price movements of up to 25% or more, *for no pressing economic reason.* However, I have also found that a feedback-loop movement does not last much more than 13 weeks maximum in a decline and about 26 weeks on an advance. These movements can be followed by another three months of stabilization.

The best example is the 1962 crash. This crash, illustrated in the graph in Figure 2.3, lasted 13 weeks. The market declined more than 25%, and there was no economic reason for it, which frightened investors and analysts even more and made the feedback action (selling out of fear) worse. The field of technical analysis attempts to understand

FIGURE 2.3   The 1962 stock market decline was a 25% movement that seems to have been nearly 100% feedback. There was little, if any, economic reason to explain it.

what causes these instabilities and how to distinguish a stable from an unstable market. The study of economic factors is incapable of locating instabilities because the cause of the extreme movement is not found in economics. After the 1962 crash, the market made bottom, stabilized, and started on a 3-year advance to new highs.

The idea is not new that stock market price movements often exhibit characteristics similar to those in physical systems with feedback loops. Many people have fitted feedback loops into their ideas and many models allow for it. What is somewhat new is the discovery that these loops can sometimes grow much larger than academics originally assumed, but this finding has been incorporated into the newest models. However, it is my opinion that even with these allowances, current theories still don't model the stock market correctly—something important is missing. I believe what they're missing is that feedback in the market is not one loop but three separate loops. The market's price action is a manifestation of the concurrent and overlapping action of all three loops. This idea becomes clearer after examining a concept that I call the time intention of the trade.

THE TIME INTENTION OF THE TRADE

I believe that understanding and then categorizing investors by what I call the *time intention of the trade* helps illuminate stock market price movements and is fundamental to understanding any stock market model. It is interesting that Wall Street has no real definition of this concept. The term *investor's time horizon* (the period through which a person can invest before he or she needs the money) is close but not really the same. *Time intention of the trade* means that an investor has a clear idea of the expected length of time between the purchase date and the sale date of an investment even before the investment has begun.

In truth, the stock market is not one investment activity but the sum of many, each categorized by the time intention of the trade. For example, some investors try to predict and profit from short-term price movements that last from a day to a few weeks: They buy today with the intention of selling in a few days. They live in a very small time world, where hours often seem like years. In that world, a sharp 2-day sell-off is a bear market and something to be avoided. Then there are intermediate-term investors, who focus on price movements lasting a month to many months. Their time world or scale is much larger. The third category is the long-term investor, who focuses on movements of many months to a few years.

Each of these investment activities, defined and categorized by the time intention of the trade, is a legitimate investment activity in its own realm. I am not attempting to evaluate whether an investment strategy applied to any one period is more correct than another—I simply acknowledge their existence and effects. The price movements we see every day and all the activity that makes up the daily tape is the sum of all the different time worlds going on concurrently. Wall Street has always talked about short-, intermediate-, and long-term traders, but the concept has never been seen as a fundamental and illuminating idea. When its importance is recognized, and the idea of unstable markets

---

The **time intention of the trade** is the time—measured in minutes, days, weeks, or months—between the start of a transaction and its intended conclusion. It is a clear statement of the expected duration of the investment.

due to feedback loops is also considered, a realistic model for stocks emerges.

I distinctly remember the event that brought this to the fore in my mind. In the summer of 1973, I was visiting the floor of the Pacific Coast Stock Exchange on Spring Street, Los Angeles. I struck up a conversation with the floor specialist in Alza Corporation. The day's trading was over, he was wrapping things up, and I said something like, "The market's starting to look pretty good." He disagreed and said he was nervous. We talked a little more, but the conversation was strange. Every time he said something, I became puzzled. When I said, "Well, with the market so oversold . . ." he curtly interrupted with a disagreeing look and said, "What do you mean oversold? It was up 15 points yesterday and 20 points today [those were big moves back then]—the market is extremely overbought."

I went silent as I realized why we hadn't been communicating: We had been discussing two completely different things. Although we had experienced the exact same stock market each day, we had experienced it differently; we were thinking and living in two completely different time worlds.

At that time I was interested in the intermediate-term movement of the market. Since stocks had been declining for 4 months, it was oversold in my world. The specialist, however, was involved in every trade of the day. He was focused on the minute-to-minute fluctuations. To him the market was overbought; it had gone up 2 days in a row! He was so far removed from what was happening in the intermediate term that it didn't exist for him. It's like an elephant and an ant walking around on the same hill. The ant is walking into a small crevice of the hill and that crevice is all it sees. The elephant doesn't even see the crevice, only the big hill. The ant can see only the crevice, while the elephant focuses on the characteristics and shape of the hill—yet they are experiencing the same hill!

As I drove home, I couldn't get this realization out of my mind. What hit me as the important point was that all these different investment activities, categorized by the time scale of interest, existed together coincidental in time, seemingly independent of one another. It was a mistake to think that short-term trading was unimportant and that long-term investing was the only important area. With feedback loops, price action in one time frame can magnify and affect another.

Although this idea was to find its way eventually into my model of the market, it had a more immediate and useful application in solving a paradox I had noticed. As mentioned earlier, in 1974, market technicians were using specialist data (buys, sells, and short sells) to forecast long-term market moves. If my insight here was correct, however, this couldn't be—the specialist wasn't interested in and didn't act in that time frame. Nonetheless, the indicators developed using specialist data had a fantastic record of correctly signaling major long-term tops and bottoms. How could they be so successful? I'll explain how in Chapter 5.

Short-Term Trading Is Important

You might think that short-term trading is less important than long-term investing. However, if you look at the amount of money invested by short-term traders (e.g., specialists, floor traders, day traders) you find that it represents about 30% of daily volume or more, and this is a rather large percent. You might say, "Yes, but these traders produce short-term price moves that last a day or two and can be ignored." Wrong! Here is where chaos theory and the power of feedback loops show that short-term traders may be able to trigger a movement that can carry on for weeks.

Each group of investors, grouped by the time intention of their trading, can generate feedback-loop movements in that time frame. For example, short-term traders can become nervous and produce extremely fast, but short-term, price changes. Certain instabilities can also exist in the minds of intermediate-term traders that, when triggered, can produce extremely fast intermediate-term price changes. Finally, instabilities can exist in the minds of long-term traders that can influence longer-term price changes.

Long-term trader instability is much less important than the first two because the mechanism behind the feedback loops lies in emotional reactions of the participants, and it is difficult to hold an emotion and react to it over a long period. In fact, I have never seen a feedback-loop decline last longer than 13 weeks. On the other hand, positive feedback loops—instabilities that drive prices higher than economics justifies—seem to be able to carry forward to extremes for up to 6 months.

The Market's Three Feedback Loops
and the 1987 Crash: A Feedback Loop Deluxe

The feedback loop of the stock market is not one loop but three. Investors grouped by the time intention of their trading (short, intermediate and long term) and reacting to price movements of a certain size in

FIGURE 2.4   The 1987 stock market crash was a feedback loop deluxe. Program trading accentuated stock price movements, which triggered the feedback loops of all three time domains—short, intermediate, and long term—in one day. Regulations on program trading that were created after the crash, called *collars*, were intended to help keep program trading from ever acting as an extreme feedback trigger again.

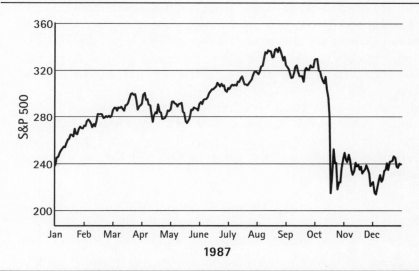

their time domains, can generate a feedback loop for that domain. These three time worlds act somewhat independently of one another, as separate domains, but at times they influence one another. The 1987 crash, in which programmed trading magnified price movements out of all proportion, was an example of all three feedback loops being triggered simultaneously.

The 1987 crash, shown in Figure 2.4, caught everyone by surprise, including me. There was no fundamental economic problem to trigger it. Selling, magnified by programmed trading, triggered an underlying instability that in turn created more instability, and down the market went. The boards of governors of the major exchanges know the theories about feedback loops and emotional selling, and after the crash, they set up price and program trading limits to prevent the bleed-over effect from happening again.

The Advisor Frozen in the TV Lights

For a long time, I'll be remembered in the Los Angeles area as the stock market commentator who was on the air early Monday morning, October 27, 1987, at the local financial station and who became a little rattled trying to explain what was happening. I'm not a professional announcer, but I appeared on television once a week to offer my investment opinions. My normal routine was to jot down some notes in the car on the way to the studio and put them in my top pocket so I'd have something interesting to tell viewers on my first update. The notes covered something I read about the market over the weekend. I usually did the first market commentary 15 minutes after the market opening and, with a foggy Monday morning mind, counted on these notes to get me through. Later, I would assess the market and the news background for more current observations.

At the studio, I put on my microphone and sat down in front of the large number board; I was to be on in 2 minutes. I immediately saw that the Dow Jones was down 140 points (that would be 600 points today) and it had been open only 15 minutes. I asked the cameraman what was going on. He didn't know. I took my microphone off, ran over to the general manager, and asked him what was going on. He said, "I don't know—you're supposed to know." I said, "You're right." I ran back to the board, put on the mike as the lights and camera came on, and I gave my usual pleasant, "Good morning."

I started to go over the market statistics, beginning with the number of advancing and declining issues. As I recall, it was something like 1,400 stocks declining and 7 advancing. The amount of advancing volume was so small it wasn't even registering on the Quotron board. I almost stopped and said that the Quotron board was broken, but I wasn't sure, so I just kept going. Near the end, when I would normally start thinking about what I was going to say, my mind went onto to my notes. I realized with horror that they were completely useless. What was I going to do, just ignore all this and talk about some irrelevant observation from the weekend? I didn't know the cause of the crash—maybe some terrible national event had occurred to trigger it.

Suddenly, the dreaded thought came that I had nothing to say. I froze. When the camera returned to me, I simply stared ahead, sweating and speechless, for 10 seconds. Eventually I said something in a squeaky, panicked voice and it was over.

It took me about a half hour to calm down and compose myself. When I came back for the next update, I said the decline looked like a selling climax. I was right, but the bottom was 4 hours and 400 points (another 15%) away. Neither I nor anyone else had ever seen a one-day market decline so severe.

Feedback Loops and Market News

Investors usually estimate the importance of an economic news item by what happens to the market after the news is released. What seems to be a minor news item can act like the bird in the example of the avalanche— as a trigger—setting off an unstable market and thereby causing a huge price movement way out of proportion to the importance of the news. Therefore, when a strong feedback-loop move is in play, it is very hard to evaluate the real import of any news. Is the market reacting because the economic news is really that bad, or has an instability just been triggered?

During these moments, investors can become very confused. They wake up in the morning and hear some news that doesn't seem too bad. As they watch the market begin a major sell-off, seemingly way out of proportion to the news, they might think, "Boy, did I figure that wrong! I must be missing something important here." No longer confident in what they know, they often join the selling, deciding to sidestep the market until they can figure it out again. Sometimes they have missed something important, but often they have just failed to understand the feedback-loop mechanism in stock prices.

Investor uncertainty can work in another way—analysts and the media can start inventing economic reasons to explain what is in truth only a strong feedback-loop price movement. Although the 1987 crash was really just an extreme feedback loop, for months afterward many people were convinced we were heading into a severe recession. They needed a strong economic reason to explain what had just happened, but having nothing available, they started inventing ideas. Articles began appearing on the cover of the *Wall Street Journal* tracing the outline of the 1987 crash against the 1929 crash, predicting severe economic problems. There was nothing to support the recession theory, however, except the market crash itself. Eventually, the market did recover, as investors regained confidence and there was no recession.

Understanding that feedback loops exist all by themselves is a major step to understanding some large stock price movements. It doesn't make the loss of money any less painful or the uncertainty any less, but it can help you understand what you are up against. It can also open up a person's mind to consider other factors besides economics when forecasting in unstable markets.

The Time Intention of the Trade Clarifies Many Things

Besides bringing some clarity to the structure of the market's feedback loops, the time intention of the trade, which is really an effort to compartmentalize investors by their time focus, helps clarify many confusing areas of investing. For one, knowing the time intention of a trade helps clarify the type of financial information an investor or speculator will study.

Although it might seem trivial and something everyone should know, it is seldom addressed. The question is very simple: "What type of information should you study if you want to correctly time the market?" This question can be posed, but can't be answered until we know the time intention of the trade. This is because you use different tools and consider different information depending on the expected period of your investment. Short-term traders usually study some type of technical analysis, whereas longer-term investors usually study the economic picture of a company (you'll learn about these two types of information in Chapters 3 and 4).

Without knowing the time intention of a trade, an investor doesn't know what to study. A great deal of trader and investor confusion stems from this one vital point. Without clear definitions of the time frame, investor activity often becomes illogical. For example, an investor decides to buy a stock because of long-term earnings growth. When the price drops 10% in two weeks, she decides to sell, although the stock's earnings prospects haven't changed at all. She bought the stock based on data that predicts long-term movement and then sold because of data used to trade shorter-term movements. This investor had not clearly defined the time intention of the trade.

Another reason the time intention of the trade is so important has to do with the concept of stock market predictability. The efficient market theory says that the market is random and unpredictable, like the flipping of a coin. In my experience (and that of many others), the market is not always random but is sometimes predictable. The model presented in the next section allows for this.

If you accept that the market is sometimes predictable, you must ask an important question: "How long does it stay predictable before it slips into its normal random and unpredictable state?" Another important question is "When the market does become predictable, what size and time duration of price moves does it usually predict: short, intermediate, or long term?" Shouldn't an investor's time intention of the trade match the time scale over which the market seems to be predictable?

It is my conclusion, supported by a study discussed in Chapter 5, that stock market movements lasting from 3 to 6 months are the ones that are relatively predictable. Only under unusual circumstances can longer-term movements be predicted with a high degree of certainty.

THE STOCK MARKET MODEL I USE

You are now ready to see the model that I believe is a closer representation of the real stock market than any other. Before you do, however, one final piece is missing. There must be a term for fair value.

A major feedback-loop movement, even though it can cause an advance or decline of 25% or more for no economic reason, should not be confused with a bull or bear market. In my opinion, to be called a bull or bear market, a movement should have some long-term economic reason behind it and should last at least 9 months to a couple of years. Because feedback loops can't last more than about 13 weeks maximum (with up to another 3 months of adjusting to it), real bull and bear markets are usually composed of a sequence of feedback-loop movements. The market goes from unstable to stable, where it sits for a while, until deteriorating or constructive economic forces bring about a new instability, which leave it vulnerable to the next triggering event. There is always an economic or financial reason behind a movement of that duration.

Any accurate model of the stock market must contain economic factors, and they must be of primary importance. Technical analysis aside, long-term stock market movements do reflect financial and economic conditions, and markets do move up and down long term because of perceived changes in the economic picture. In my model, the term that represents this economic factor is the term for fair value. To symbolize fair value, I use the mathematical expression D/I, where D stands for dividends and I stands for interest rates. (This term is more fully explained in Chapter 3.)

The complete model is shown in Figure 2.5. According to the model, stock prices equal a fair value modified and stretched by the action of the three somewhat independent feedback loops of three time domains. This model, with its inclusion of the feedback loops, opens the door to a sometimes predictable market. These four factors have a dynamic interplay that ultimately causes the wiggling price movements you see in stock charts.

FIGURE 2.5   A schematic of the stock market model I use. The price of a stock equals a fair value (D/I) modified and stretched by the action of three somewhat independent feedback loops of different time domains.

The Stock Market Model I Use

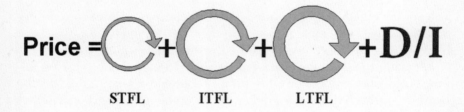

STFL   ITFL   LTFL

Key

STFL - Short Term Feedback Loop

ITFL - Intermediate Term Feedback Loop

LTFL - Long Term Feedback Loop

D/I - Fair Value Term

MARKET PREDICTABILITY

The efficient market theory says that the future course of stocks is un-predictable, like the flipping of a coin: The chances of being right at any given time are 50 : 50. From my experience, this is true most of the time. At other times, however, it is not true, and the market is highly pre-dictable. When I say that the market at certain times is predictable, I mean that the odds of correctly forecasting market direction are at times better than 50 : 50.

How can this be, since there is no way to know the unexpected eco-nomic news that drives the market? Because those feedback loops are sometimes very predictable. It may be impossible to predict the next economic statistic, but I believe it is sometimes possible to know when a market has become unstable and when a feedback loop might be triggered.

How do you describe or define an activity that is completely unpre-dictable some of the time and at other times somewhat predictable? Is there any analogy with some system whose predictability ebbs and flows from random to somewhat predictable? Yes, there is. My analogy might make you uncomfortable at first, but keep in mind that it's only an example of a system with changing odds; no other relationship with the stock market is implied. The analogous situation is the game of blackjack.

In blackjack, there are certain odds, say 52 : 48, that the house will win. However, the odds aren't fixed at those numbers; they *average* 52 : 48. At times, the odds are even greater in the house's favor, and at other times, the odds go the other way and favor the players. This is true be-cause the initial odds of 52 : 48 depend on the ratio of the number of 10-cards to non-10-cards in a standard 52-card deck. If, in the first deal, a disproportionate number of 10-cards comes out, the ratio shifts for the remaining deck. This is the essence of card counting—trying to deter-mine when a deck is out of balance in favor of the bettor. With the stock market, it is a much more difficult proposition (Figure 2.6).

Suppose that a similar situation exists with the stock market. Assume that the stock market is usually a 50 : 50 proposition, but at certain times these odds shift and the direction of prices becomes more predictable: 60 : 40, for example. What do you look for to see that the market is now in your favor, that it is more likely to go either up or down? This is a very

FIGURE 2.6   A schematic diagram showing that the stock market is usually random and unpredictable but at times shifts into periods when it can become very predictable.

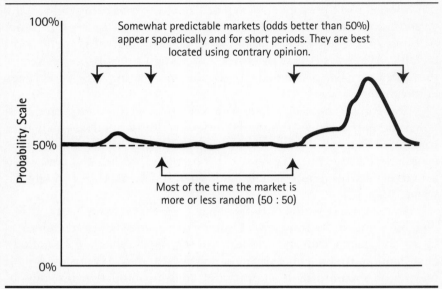

important question and one that I try to answer in the remainder of the book.

Before we go forward, let's take a look at one of the greatest traders in American stock market history, Jesse Livermore. After 50 years of trading, he reached a similar conclusion regarding the predictability of the stock market.

Jesse Livermore

Jesse Livermore was one of the great stock speculators of Wall Street. Legend has it that he made four million-dollar fortunes over a trading career that lasted 50 years, from 1890 to 1940. His first job at age 12 was posting prices for customers who were placing bets in a local stock market bucket shop. Soon he was placing bets himself and winning. In a few months, he had earned $1,000. He became so successful that all the bucket shops banned his activities. He then began speculating in stocks and eventually became successful at that, too. Stock speculation was the only job Livermore ever had.

Over time, he matured from a short-term tape reader to a speculator who planned his operations based on longer-term economic trends. He made his first million in 1906, which also saw the start of a massive credit crunch and stock market decline that he foresaw. After losing some of his nest egg in three short positions taken a little too soon, his fourth short position was right on target, eventually yielding him millions in profits as the market crashed. He bought the shares back at the bottom of the market and acquired the name of Boy Wonder.

Many books were written about him, the most famous being the 1917 *Reminiscences of a Stock Operator*, by Edwin Lefevre. It may be the most well-known book ever written on the subject of stock speculation, and it's still in print today. In his own book, *How to Trade in Stocks*, Livermore said, "One cannot be successful by speculating every day or every week. There are only a few times a year, possibly four or five, when you should allow yourself to make a commitment at all. In the interim you are letting the market shape itself for the next big move."

He lost most of his money in the 1929 crash and never really made it back in the heavily regulated environment that followed.

Now that we have defined the model I use to understand how stock prices behave, the next few chapters explore the two disciplines—technical and fundamental analysis—that are used to study the two components of the model. Technical analysis is concerned with the study of stable and unstable markets, including the three feedback loops. Fundamental analysis is the study of the D/I term that defines fair value. The first subject under consideration is the fair value term and the theory behind it.

3

Fair Value: The Theory of Stacking the Money

A s discussed in the first chapter, the accepted efficient market model concludes that stock prices are essentially random and unpredictable. This presents us, however, with the amusing picture of thousands of people on Wall Street trying to do everyday what a widely accepted theory says can't be done—predict stock prices. The new model for stock prices, presented in the last chapter, I believe is more accurate and much closer to the ideas most traders have about stocks, and allows for a stock market that can sometimes be predicted, thus saving Wall Street the embarrassment of contradicting itself every day.

Figure 3.1 shows this new model, which says that the price of a stock equals a fair-value term modified and stretched by three feedback loops working over three time domains. Fair value is represented symbolically by the term D/I, where D stands for dividends and I for interest rates. If you think dividends no longer have meaning in today's stock market, you should pay close attention. Throughout this chapter, you will see why dividends and interest rates are so important, or at least should be, to stock prices.

A major bull or bear market—or any price movement lasting longer than nine months—always requires an economic reason for its occurrence. A long trading range market like the one I'm expecting should last

---

FIGURE 3.1   In this stock market model, the price of a stock is a fair-value term modified and stretched by the action of short-, intermediate-, and long-term feedback loops. The term for fair value is *D/I*, which is symbolic. It is really the sum of a long series of fractions, in which each fraction is a future dividend divided by an increasing power of the current interest rate (*D* divided by *I*).

The Stock Market Model I Use

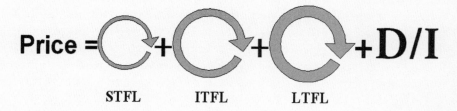

$$\text{Price} = \circlearrowright + \circlearrowright + \circlearrowright + D/I$$

STFL   ITFL   LTFL

Key

STFL - Short Term Feedback Loop

ITFL - Intermediate Term Feedback Loop

LTFL - Long Term Feedback Loop

D/I - Fair Value Term

---

a number of years, so the reasons for it are fundamental, not technical. To understand what the economic factors might be, you need to learn more about the fair-value term of the model.

FAIR VALUE

The theory behind the fair-value term in the model is simple. It is an old theory that says that the current price of a stock should exactly equal the present value of all that company's future dividends. This chapter explains the theory and how it applies to today's stocks. Your initial reaction may be that this statement can't be true because you know many companies that have never paid a dividend and yet still have a stock price.

Nevertheless, as you will see, the model still holds. As we explore the idea behind *D/I*, you will learn how stocks with no current dividend can have a theoretical stock price.

WHY FAIR VALUE THEORY IS NOT WELL KNOWN

I must confess that I studied the stock market for more than 20 years before I knew what fair value was or that there was even a formula for it. I found it much easier to study technical analysis. I was more interested in intermediate-term price movements lasting about six months and I found that technical, not fundamental analysis seemed to work better for forecasting prices in that time frame. I also found most of the instruc-

Bridging the Math Problem

People who haven't studied mathematics often have strange ideas about it. Many think that scientists work long hours on complicated equations looking for some deep formula that contains a great truth of nature, yet this is far from what they really do. Most scientists don't think in terms of mathematics; they think in terms of concepts and use mathematics only to test these concepts. In real life, mathematicians and physicists often get very sloppy with their calculations, doing quick tricks that would upset a strict math teacher. These scientists have come to know that mathematics is really only a tool (and a marvelous one) to obtain insights into how things work. They are familiar enough with the tools of their trade (math symbols) that they know when to be exact and when they can be sloppy and still get a close answer.

The famous physicist Richard Feynman used to revel in his ability to explain very complicated physics theories without using any mathematics while not losing any of the theory's truths. He could do this since he had learned that real insight usually stands on the other side of the mathematics. This typically comes after immersing oneself in the mathematics, then finding the two or three core ideas that come out of it. He would pull these out, bypassing the mathematics, and show the reader how simple it all is.

Feynman's book called *QED (Quantum ElectroDynamics)* demonstrated how everything we experience in the universe can be explained by the act of combining, in an infinite variety of ways, three basic actions. Behind all the math lay that simple truth. Amazing.

The average reader, hearing only these simple truths and not seeing any complex equations, often thinks he or she is getting the cheap explanation—the great truths must lie somewhere deep inside the math. But this is not so.

The same is true on a much simpler scale about the fair value of stocks. It is usually presented in complex mathematical form, which has confused many readers. Baffled by mathematical symbolism just out of reach, they often think that understanding fair value is beyond them. I will therefore sidestep the mathematics and try to show you the few practical truths buried inside it.

tional books written to explain theories of stock valuation were poorly written and often confusing.

It wasn't until I had to study the intricacies of the bond market that I finally came into possession of the basic underlying ideas that govern the evaluation of almost all financial assets, including the stock market. I then began to understand why these basic ideas seldom make it down to the popular level of investing and, in truth, are not well known by many professional investors. The reason is simple: The ideas are just mathematical enough to be beyond the understanding of 95% of most people who try to study them.

I'm quite serious. A few years ago, I was at a meeting with more than 50 stockbrokers in which the speaker promised $100 to anyone who could explain how bond prices are calculated and the exact theory behind it. No one won the $100. Everyone parroted the simple, short-cut formulas they were taught in class but they couldn't really explain the underlying theory. Believe me, if you don't know how a bond is priced, you have no idea of how stocks are valued. I realized that concepts like fair value for stocks and bonds require a slightly higher level of math comprehension than most people seem to have. If the subject is approached in a slightly different manner, however, this general problem can be sidestepped.

THE FUNDAMENTALS: TIME AND MONEY

A Dollar Today Is . . .

We have all heard the following statement: "A dollar today is worth more than a dollar tomorrow." Everyone agrees with this simple statement, but few know that all of finance theory rests on fully understanding exactly what it means. Behind that simple statement lies everything there is to know about stocks and bonds.

If you're asked, "Why is a dollar today worth more than a dollar tomorrow?" you would probably say, "Because of inflation. A dollar buys more today than it will in the future." In fact, this is wrong; inflation has nothing to do with it. During periods of deflation, a dollar actually buys less today than it will tomorrow, so if the statement is a universal truth for all time, inflation can't be the answer.

Whether you have inflation or deflation, a dollar today is still worth more than a dollar tomorrow. If inflation is not the reason, why is a dollar today worth more than one tomorrow? It is true for the same reason a 10-year-old child is smarter than a newborn baby: The older child has lived 10 years longer and has had the opportunity to accumulate and learn more information. Similarly, a dollar earned 10 years ago has been "living" 10 years longer than a dollar received today. During those 10 years, the older dollar has had more time to accumulate to itself some interest income. This is true regardless of inflation or deflation.

How do financial people compare the value of two dollars earned at two different moments in time? They calculate how much interest the earlier dollar would compound to itself during the period before the future dollar is earned. The interest rate used in this calculation is usually the safest interest rate available for the time period in question.

Let's try this out. Let us compare a dollar earned today versus a dollar to be earned 10 years from now. Suppose the 10-year interest rate is

7.17%. If we take the dollar today and compound it for 10 years at 7.17%, in 10 years we have $2. So the dollar today will be $2 in 10 years—it is twice as large as that future dollar.

We can also go the other way in time. We could bring that future dollar into the present and see how it compares to the dollar today. Doing the calculation in reverse, we find that that future dollar is worth only 50 cents today. A future dollar's current value is often called its *present value*.

From this simple idea comes a very simple rule: You can only compare dollars if you bring them all to the same moment in time. If an expected stream of dollars is to be earned, you have to bring all those dollars to the same moment in time to add, subtract, or compare them in any way. The simple formula that allows you to bring any future dollar into present time is this:

$$\text{A future dollar's present value} = \$1/(1 + I)^T$$

where I is the interest rate and T is the time between the two dollars.

The entire subject of finance, stocks, bonds, and so on is built on this simple equation.

An Important Conclusion

Let's carefully inspect this equation and see what simple truths come out of it. We assumed an interest rate of 7.17% and the present value of that dollar to be earned in 10 years is 50 cents today. Suppose, however, that tomorrow, because of some dramatic economic news, interest rates plunge. They go from 7.17% to 5%. We go to our formula and recalculate what the present value of that dollar is the next day. We do the calculation and find that that future dollar, instead of being worth 50 cents as it was yesterday, now has a present value of 61 cents. In other words, in one day, the present value of that future dollar has jumped 22%, from 50 cents to 61 cents.

This startles most people because they look around and the world looks pretty much the same. Yet this is what the theory says. Now, if the interest rate had gone up from 7.17% to 9% in one day, the opposite would have occurred. In that event, the dollar to be paid in 10 years, instead of being valued at 50 cents, is now worth only 42 cents. This simple but slightly strange conclusion is an extremely important one.

Another Important Factor

Can this simple equation account for all the complexity we see in the world of finance? Not quite. One more idea is required. We must somehow mathematically allow for another factor—the uncertainty of knowing the exact future. For example, we might be expecting a dollar to come our way in 10 years, but maybe the payee of that dollar won't be there to make it. He or she could die or go out of business. A term must be included in the formula that allows for this.

Let us call that term P. P is a number that represents the probability that you will receive that future dollar. $P = 1$ means that the payment of that future dollar is 100% guaranteed. $P = .5$ represents a 50 : 50 chance of payment, and $P = 0$ means you are guaranteed not to get it.

Taking this factor into account, the complete formula is this:

$$\text{A future dollar's present value} = P \,^\circ\, \$1/(1 + I)^T$$

where I is the interest rate, T is the time between the two dollars, and P is a number between 1 and 0 that reflects the probability that future dollar will be paid.

Let us consider again the example of the dollar to be paid in 10 years if interest rates are 7.17%. We already know that that dollar is worth 50 cents today. Suppose we also know that in 10 years, when it is to be paid, someone will flip a coin and only pay the dollar if the coin comes up heads. Since there is only a 50 : 50 chance of getting paid the dollar, that future dollar is really worth 25 cents. If you want to buy that future dollar, you shouldn't pay more than 25 cents for it today.

Now we are in a position to understand what fair value is and how it is calculated. As mentioned earlier, the current price of a stock should exactly equal the present value of all that company's future dividends. That statement probably means more now than it did earlier. Before we get into exactly what it means, I first want to apply what we know to two simple situations to get a feel for the how the rules are applied. The first example is how to calculate what is known as a lump sum pension.

Applying the Money Rules to Calculate a Lump Sum Pension

A few years ago, I was asked to develop a customized retirement seminar for TRW corporation. This company allows employees the option of taking their pensions as either a lump sum payment or a monthly check paid over life. In this seminar, I had to teach these retirees exactly what a lump sum pension was and, because many of the employees were scientists, I was able to expand the presentation and explain the concept with a little more mathematics. In the process of trying to find the right level of mathematics to communicate the meaning of the term *lump sum*, I realized the importance of the underlying presentation in terms of understanding stock values.

Theoretically, a lump sum pension payment is the amount that pension actuaries think is *exactly* equal to what the pensioner would receive if she or he chose the monthly-check-for-life option. How does a pension actuary make this calculation? It's a two-step process. Figure 3.2 illustrates the first step.

The first step in the process of calculating a lump sum payment is to determine the present value of each year's pension payments. Let's assume that a retiree's current age is 62, with a lifetime pension of $1,000

FIGURE 3.2   The first step in calculating a lump sum pension is to calculate the present value of all future pension payments.

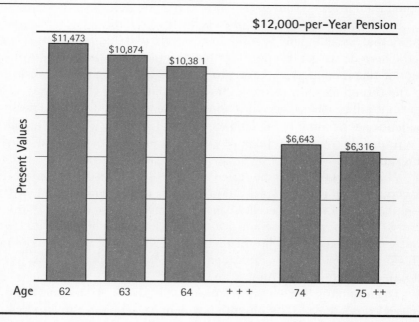

per month, or $12,000 a year. First, we get a calculator, a piece of paper, and a stubby pencil. With these simple tools, we can calculate the present value of each $12,000 yearly payment.

As we now know, the present value is the amount you need *today*, so if it was compounded, it would grow to each future $12,000 payment. To make this calculation, of course, you need an interest rate to compound with. Federal law requires that pension actuaries use the 30-year Treasury bond interest rate. As of this writing, the current 30-year T-bond interest rate is 5.06%, so we will use that figure in our calculations.

Now that we have our interest rate, let's calculate some specific present values. For example, what amount of money would grow to $12,000 in 13 years (for age 75)? Using my calculator and stubby pencil, I figure that at 5.06% we'd need $6,316 today. In other words, $6,316 will grow to $12,000 in 13 years at 5.06%.

A pension actuary would make this same calculation for every year from age 62 to age 110. Yes, age 110! (These pension actuaries take their jobs very seriously.) Not much money is needed today to account for that payment at age 110. In fact, according to my calculations, the present value for $12,000 when the retiree is 110 is $1,122. After we have calculated all the present values, we make a list of them with our stubby pencil and then proceed to step two.

In step two, we take each present value and multiply it by the probability that the company is going to have to make that payment. Where in the heck do we get this number? From actuarial studies—those amazing documents that predict the probability of a person at any age living to any future age. For example, there's about a 65% chance that a 62-year-old will be alive at age 75. Therefore, we would multiply the present value for age 75, that being $6,316, by .65. The result ($4,105) is called the probability-weighted present value of a $12,000 payment at age 75 (Figure 3.3).

We then make this same calculation for each present value, all the way to age 110. For example, the probability of being alive at age 110 is less than 1%, so the probability-weighted present value at age 110 is less than $10. Then we mathematically stack these probability-weighted present values on top of each other—in other words, we add them all up. This sum is the lump sum equivalent of the monthly pension checks for life. In our example, the lump sum is $148,673.

To an actuary, these two are equal: that is, the lump sum of $148,673 exactly equals the $1,000-a-month payment for life. You can also look at it from another viewpoint: If you wanted to buy a $1,000-a-month pay-

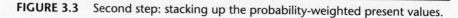

FIGURE 3.3 Second step: stacking up the probability-weighted present values.

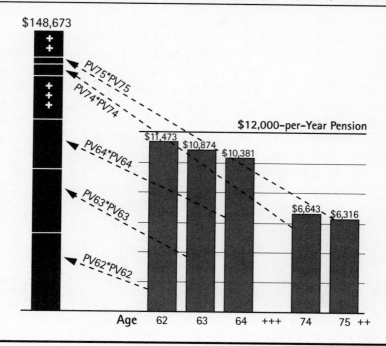

ment for life, you would have to pay $148,673 right now. (Note that another company might come up with different figures, depending on the life-expectancy tables used by the actuary.)

How Interest Rates Affect the Lump Sum

Let's play around with this concept. Suppose the retiree goes to his benefits department, learns about these two retirement payment options ($1,000 for life or $148,673 lump sum) and goes home to think about it. A few months later, he goes back and asks whether his retirement package has changed. He learns that although the monthly pension hasn't changed (it's still $1,000 per month), the lump sum is larger; it is now $151,356. The retiree is mystified, but suddenly remembers that over the last two months interest rates declined. Then it dawns on him what is going on. The lump sum is always being evaluated and calculated in the interest rate environment of that moment. In other words, *given no change in the monthly pension, the retiree is entitled to a bigger lump sum for no other reason than that interest rates are now lower.*

This is a very important conclusion: When interest rates go down, the lump sum goes up. When rates go up, the lump sum goes down. It is the same result that we saw with any single present value and is really the aggregate manifestation of this conclusion applied to the present value of the whole stack. Once employees become aware of this phenomenon, they often try to time their retirement for when they think interest rates will be at their lowest. The relationship between the size of the lump sum and interest rates is shown in Figure 3.4.

Our example of how a lump sum is calculated is very important because the same procedure is the one used to determine the price of both stocks and bonds. You probably think that there is a lot more to stock

FIGURE 3.4 When interest rates are low, lump sum pensions are high. When interest rates are high, lump sum pensions are low. Because of this, many retirees whose companies offer the lump sum pension payment try to plan their retirement when they think interest rates will be low.

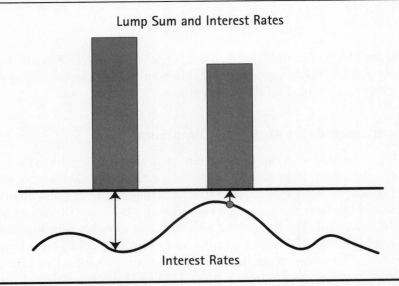

Lump Sum and Interest Rates

Interest Rates

> **Stacking the money** is what I call the mathematical procedure to find the current worth or value of any investment that will throw off a future stream of income or cash. This theory recognizes that money, like any commodity, has a value and that the current value of any investment—stocks, bonds, real estate, and so on—should be determined using this or some variation on this idea.

prices than this, but except for the feedback loops discussed in Chapter 1, there isn't. All the thinking and effort that goes into Wall Street projections boil down to calculations like the ones we just performed to figure a lump sum pension. When performing these types of calculations, analysts and actuaries say they are making calculations based on the *time value of money*. However, I think the term *stacking the money* more accurately describes the process, because the calculations involve stacking one number on top of another to get the total value. I call it the stacking the money theory.

Remember: When interest rates rise, the lump sum gets smaller. When they go down, the lump sum gets bigger. Does any of this sound familiar? Have you ever heard that high interest rates are bad for stock and bond prices and low interest rates make them go up? Do you think there is a relationship between why the lump sum pension goes up or down and why stocks and bonds also go up and down when interest rates change?

STACKING THE MONEY TO DETERMINE BOND PRICES

Stacking the money is the only theory used to calculate bond prices. Let's take a look at how it works. Suppose you have a U.S. Treasury bond with 10 years left to maturity. The bond has an 8% coupon, so it pays $80 per year to the holder for the next 9 years, and in the tenth year it will pay the final $80, as well as the face value on the bond ($1,000 in this case).

What's a fair price for this bond today? First, we need to look up the current Treasury interest rate in the free market. We use this rate to

FIGURE 3.5 The price of a bond is calculated following the same stacking-the-money procedure used for calculating a lump sum pension payment.

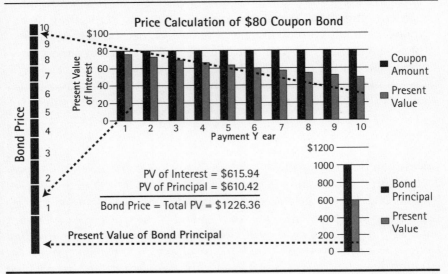

calculate the present value of each $80 payment for the next 10 years, as well as the present value of the final $1,000 payment (Figure 3.5). Unlike with lump sum pension payments, the probability that payments might not be made isn't an issue because the government guarantees the payments. This removes the probability factor from the equation. Finally, you stack (in other words, add up) all these values to determine the price of the bond.

Bond prices rise and fall with interest rates for the same reason the lump sum pension rises and falls. In fact, after a bond is issued and its coupon is fixed, all a bond's price ever does is march to changing interest rates—that is, its price adjusts daily to reflect the ever-changing interest rate environment it lives in. With bonds, the link between interest rates and the price of a bond, just like the lump sum, is immediate and direct. Stocks follow the same theory, but here the connection is looser because with stocks, the payments you'll be stacking are fuzzy numbers.

NOTE

By the way, when calculating corporate bonds (where there is a possibility of default), the probability factor is not 1. Instead, you must multiply the present values for each coupon plus the principal payments by a number that represents the chance of default for that particular coupon. You then stack these default probability-weighted present values to find the price of the bond. Whether you are calculating bonds or stocks, you always use the safest interest rate in the formulas. The uncertainty of any payment (coupon, dividend) is allowed for by the *P* factor, not by inserting a riskier interest rate in the denominator.

STACKING THE MONEY TO DETERMINE STOCK PRICES

Now let's turn to stocks. What is the price of a stock? The same rules apply, except this time we stack dividends. The rule of the game is that you always stack what is paid out. We return to the definition of fair value for a stock: *The price for a stock should exactly equal the present value of all the company's future dividends.*

Are there any other considerations? Some time ago, I encountered the following opinion about the dividend model: To determine a company's value, patents, brand names, and other intangible assets should be valued and used with the dividend discount model. A better valuation results from adding intangibles to the model's calculation.

I disagree with this. I believe the statement for fair value is complete and sufficient unto itself and needs nothing else. Including a term like intangible assets to the equation is what engineers and scientists often call adding a fudge factor. Our model for stock prices is not a fair-value term plus three feedback loops plus a wild fudge factor. If anything, you should try to calculate how these intangibles might increase the dividends of the company. In other words, all other factors should be included only in estimating future dividends. If it is determined that these intangibles probably won't affect the future dividends of the company, then according to the model, they have no importance (if

John Burr Williams

John Burr Williams was the first man to clearly formulate a theory on how to value stocks. His theory, that a company's stock should equal the present value of its future dividends, was developed as a doctoral thesis at Harvard and eventually published in 1938, in *The Theory of Investment Value*. It is hard to believe that until this book came out, investors had no real theory on how stocks should be priced, even though the New York Stock Exchange was more than 140 yeas old.

John Williams' undergraduate education was in mathematics and chemistry, which gave him the tools and the training to approach subjects from a quantitative mindset. He later put that education to good use. After some training in business forecasting, he went to Wall Street in the mid-1920s and worked for the old brokerage firm of Hayden, Stone as a security analyst. He watched as the stock market ran up in the speculative flurry of the late 1920s and then witnessed firsthand the Great Crash of 1929 to 1932.

While other men walked away demoralized and beaten, Williams went back to Harvard determined to understand what had happened. How could stock prices go to such unbelievable levels and then, in three years, plummet? Somewhere, stocks had to have some true value, and he set about uncovering how to calculate it. Working from Irving Fisher's book, *The Theory of Interest*, published around 1900, Williams found the underlying concept that, when applied to stock prices, led to his basic theory.

The fundamental idea of calculating the present value of a future stream of money (earnings, dividends, etc.) and then adding them all up is still the basic theory used today. If you study almost any modern theory of stock evaluation and look for the fundamental theory behind it, you will find John Burr Williams' seminal ideas, formulated some 70 years ago.

there is a final liquidation or merger of a company, this would constitute a final dividend).

The model says that you take all the dividends that the stock will ever pay, calculate their present value using the current interest rate, and stack them up. The total should be the current price of the stock. Although this is feasible with bonds and pension payments, doing this calculation with stock prices involves the uncertainty of knowing what those dividend payments will be. You may know what the dividend is today and have a good idea what it will be over the next few years, but can you realistically project dividends over 10 or 15 years?

Because of the uncertainty of the value of future dividends, we can consider the dividends a type of number called *fuzzy numbers*. Usually, but not always, the farther away a dividend is, the fuzzier it is. Since the present value of a fuzzy number is also a fuzzy number, so is the fair-value sum. By the way, the fact that fair value is a fuzzy number is what allows the three feedback loops to exist. How fuzzy the fair-value term is governs the size and range of the three feedback loops (Figure 3.6). Sometimes, the fair-value calculation for extremely speculative stocks is

---

FIGURE 3.6   Stock prices follow the stacking-the-money rules. *Fair value* is the sum of a long series of fractions with dividends in the top (numerator) and an interest rate raised to a power in the bottom (denominator). In this case, however, the numerators (dividends) are fuzzy numbers, and they get fuzzier the farther out in time you go. Therefore, fair value is also a fuzzy (uncertain) number.

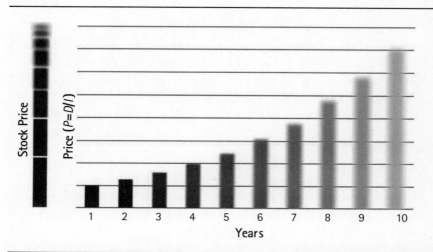

fuzzy all the way from $1 to $100, so a price movement from $5 to $20 is really nothing more than an almost 100% feedback loop movement. That describes the Internet craze of 1999 for more than 90% of the stocks involved. There is nothing wrong with playing that investment game. The problem arises when buyer and seller forget the bedrock on which the game is founded and start thinking that there is something real to the price.

In practice, to help lessen this fuzzy number problem, stock analysts use a few tricks. Instead of trying to estimate all the dividends for the next 30 years, they estimate for shorter periods, such as for 5 years. They then fold the calculation back on itself (that's the mathematical trick) and reassess these calculations as pertinent news comes in. Without going into the details of this process, assume it is the mathematical equivalent of what an explorer does when setting off for a distant land with only a compass and a map as guides. Instead of taking one compass reading and then setting off in a particular direction for good, the explorer takes the trip in stages, stopping every now and then to replot the current position. The important point to note in all this is that no matter what mathematical trick or approximation is used, behind each one is the basic concept of dividends in the numerator and interest rates in the denominator.

I don't want to explain any more details of the theory of fair value at this time. From just what I've discussed, many important conclusions can be drawn. That is what I want to focus on from this point. You'll be surprised at what you can figure out from what you've learned.

You Are at Bedrock

The theory of stacking the money shows that only two numbers go into the calculation of a stock's fair value: dividends (present and future) and the current interest rate. Other financial numbers, such as sales, market share, and costs, do not enter directly into the equation and are considered only for their ability to help determine the value of those future dividends. In other words, with this theory you are at bedrock.

Any company news or economic data has value only proportional to the degree it changes estimates for all future dividends or for the current interest rate. To the degree that investors have moved away from these basic ideas, they have moved away from investing and into the realm of speculation.

WHY INTEREST RATES ARE SO IMPORTANT

We are now in a position to understand one of the most important conclusions that comes from the stacking the money theory for fair value. We mentioned it earlier, but we return to it now since it is so important: It is the full understanding of why interest rates are so important to stock prices.

In 30 years, I have seldom heard the correct explanation of why interest rates are so important to the direction of stock prices. For example, two well-known books written by top market analysts give three reasons for the importance of interest rates.

1. Lower interest rates are good for corporate profits because they allow companies to borrow money for less.
2. Movements in interest rates make bonds more (or less) attractive compared to stocks. Lower rates makes bonds less attractive, causing people to invest more in stocks and vice versa.
3. The cost of borrowing and buying more stock, called the *margin*, is less when interest rates are low and therefore is better for stocks.

You hear the same ideas in the daily financial news when analysts talk about how the Federal Reserve board's lowering of interest rates will spur the economy. For some reason, commentators and analysts are always focusing on how the change will affect the numerators of the fractions (earnings or dividends). They never mention the really important fact—that an interest rate number goes directly into the denominators of all the fractions used to calculate stock prices, and that denominator is now smaller. As a result, investors seldom appreciate fully the impact that interest rates really do have on stock prices.

The real reason interest rates are so important to stock prices is that *the series of mathematical terms that are added up to calculate fair value have interest rates in their denominators.* Recall what you learned about fractions: When the denominator becomes smaller (interest rates go down), all the fractions get bigger (and so does fair value). When the denominator gets larger, the terms get smaller, and so does fair value. It is the same lesson we learned about the lump sum. This is the real reason interest rates are so important. When you understand this, you can see that the three previously listed reasons are really of smaller consequence. In fact, these commonly referenced ideas about why interest rates are so important actually divert attention away from this really vital point.

Fuzzy Dividends Don't Change the Interest Rate Conclusion

As we said, when you are considering the fair value of stocks, only one of the numbers in the stacking process—the interest rate—is an exact number (Figure 3.7). The other number—the dividend—is a fuzzy, or uncertain, number. These facts lead to an important conclusion: When you divide a fuzzy number by an exact number, you still get a fuzzy number. Therefore, the fair value of a stock, unlike that of a safe bond, is always fuzzy; no one knows exactly what fair value is.

That's okay—it's part and parcel of investing—but it doesn't change the conclusion of the previous section. Whether the dividends are fuzzy or not, when interest rates change overnight, these fuzzy dividends still stack to either a higher or lower number, but it is a fuzzy higher or lower number. The response in the price direction of the fuzzy number is the same as the response for the price of bonds or the lump sum pension, and it responds in the same way for the same mathematical reason.

Interest Rates and Dividends: The Yin and Yang of Stock Prices

The two factors in the equation for fair value, dividends and interest rates, give us the yin and the yang of stock prices (yin and yang because the growth of dividends and the direction of interest rates usually work opposite each other). Normally, interest rates decline as business gets bad and earnings and dividend estimates are being reduced. Similarly, interest rates go up when business expands, as earnings and dividend estimates are increased. This creates a strange situation. As dividend estimates are reduced, lower interest rates counteract the effect by increasing the present value of those reduced dividends. These movements somewhat offset each other mathematically, but not quite.

What is more important to the value of these fractions, the changing numerators or the changing denominators (i.e., lower future dividends or lower interest rates)? A mathematician would tell you that interest rates are more important because a change in interest rates today affects the calculation of the present values of every dividend, even those that will

FIGURE 3.7 Of the two numbers used to calculate fair value, one (dividends) is a fuzzy number, the other (interest rates) is an exact number. Fair value is therefore always fuzzy. This doesn't change the fact that it should rise and fall as interest rates change. The degree of fuzziness of fair value determines the size and play feedback loops will have on prices. Feedback loops can occur only if an exact, agreed-on amount for fair value doesn't exist because if it did, no one would buy or sell at any price other than the true value.

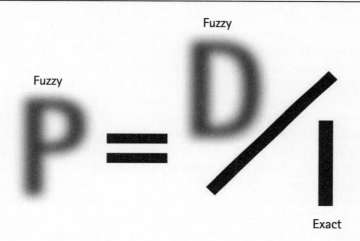

Height of Fuzzy Stack Depends on Interest Rates

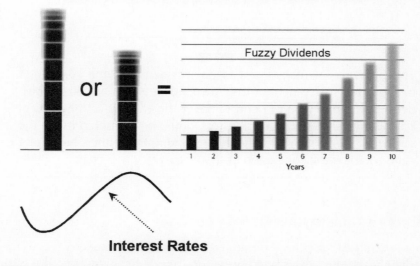

be paid 30 years from now. We saw the same thing earlier, when we watched how the present value of a dollar to be paid in 10 years can undergo a sudden increase when interest rates change. This mathematical reality is important since interest rates can and do change, sometimes by 20% in a month. On the contrary, a recession is usually expected to modify only a few years' worth of the future stream of dividends, with the farther-away dividends less affected. Only when the dividends are perceived to be in trouble for a long time (such as during the Great Depression) does the long-term reduction in dividends usually matter more than the reduction in interest rates.

This explains why stock prices often hit bottom in the worst part of the recession, when the future for business looks the worst but interest rates are declining. Many investors think that stocks start rising in the middle of a recession because farsighted investors anticipate the recovery and see expanding earnings and dividends. Yes, there is a little of that activity, but the important point is that stock prices rise because lower interest rates make the smaller dividends stack to a higher price today than they did the day before.

The tremendous importance of interest rates to stock prices can be seen in Figure 3.8. About 50% of the long-term gains in stock prices since 1982 (when the Dow Jones started its rise from just under 800), is directly attributable to the drop in interest rates from 15% to 5%. The rest of the gain is attributable to the expansion and increase in earnings and dividends.

NOTE

Today, there are many ways to pay dividends. Some companies have started to repurchase their own stock, which acts like a dividend payment. I don't intend to cover the alternative methods of paying dividends because any effect would be measured much the same way we do using the theory of stacking the money. None of it changes the basic conclusion of that theory.

Response Time to Interest Rate Changes

Theoretically, stock prices should respond to interest rate changes as immediately and directly as bond prices do. In practice, however, the difficulties involved in predicting dividends loosen the connection, and the

FIGURE 3.8   As the stacking-the-money theory indicates, about half the gains of the 18-year bull market are the result of the long drop in interest rates from 15% to 5%.

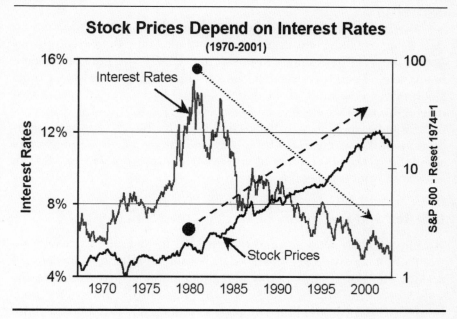

relationship is not as direct as with bonds. It is not uncommon to see both interest rates and stock prices decline simultaneously. Such a chain of events runs counter to theory. If this continues for a time, people often start saying that stock prices and interest rates have uncoupled. Although they are partially right—that is, stock prices and interest rates do occasionally break off their dance—a closer inspection reveals what is really happening. For whatever reason during these periods, investors turn their attention away from the denominator and focus entirely on the numerator. It usually happens after a severe economic event for which investors are trying to evaluate the economic ramifications.

A shift like this happened during the market decline of 1998, when a miniature currency crisis rippled through the global economy. During this crisis, American stocks experienced a 20% decline. Interest rates also declined as the crisis worsened. However, investors were so concerned about the economic repercussions on the fuzzy numbers that they didn't notice—or didn't care—that interest rates were plunging.

What had happened was that the crisis triggered feedback loops, which for a while were much more powerful than what theory was saying at the time. After the panic subsided, the theory of stacking the money took hold and prices rocketed upward.

Always pay strict attention to periods in which interest rates are either rising or falling and stock prices continue going their own way, ignoring theory. For example, in the spring of 2001, the Federal Reserve board engineered a constant decline in interest rates, and for a time, stock prices continued to decline. Commentators started saying that maybe this time the decline in rates wasn't going to stimulate the economy. When you hear that, bells should go off; they're putting your attention on the wrong part of the fraction again. At such moments, one should study the other information, such as contrary opinion, to help you figure out what is going on.

Inflation and the Theory of Stacking the Money

It's important to keep in mind that the D/I formula does not indicate whether future dividend growth occurs because of inflation or because of real growth. For example, suppose that the amount of goods a company sells remains the same, but the company increases the price of its goods by 10%. This means that the company's earnings and dividends also rise by 10%. Such an increase does not represent real growth, however, because the 10% rise is due to inflation.

By contrast, assume that inflation is zero but that sales and earnings (and eventually dividends) increase by 10%. The theory of stacking the money treats this situation identically to the situation of 10% inflation. You might think that these two should not be treated the same because one represents real expansion in business and the other doesn't, but they are treated the same—and they should be.

The difference between these two cases doesn't occur in the dividend number; it occurs in the bottom number, interest rates. During periods of inflation, interest rates are higher, and thus the dividends stack to a lower sum. In other words, if too much of a company's growth is inflation growth, a lower fair value is accorded because the interest rate (denominator) is bigger. When real growth occurs, you have the best of both worlds: high expected dividend growth and low interest rates. The theory allows for the highest possible fair value during these periods.

Applying the Model to Companies That Don't Pay Dividends

What about companies that don't pay dividends—how are their prices established? Their prices are predicated on the idea that the company will someday pay a dividend. The hope, of course, is that fantastic corporate growth will result in really big dividends in the future (Figure 3.9). After all, there is a present value for a payment, even if that payment is 10 or 15 years away. If those dividends are expected to be large enough, theory would justify a high stock price today. But if at any time investors begin to think that the company's dividends ultimately won't materialize, its stock price would go through a major evaluation.

To understand this principle, suppose that we have a time machine and go 50 years into the future. We go to a library, search the records, and discover that the small computer company named XYZ (which deals in computers, chips, software, and the Internet) grew for a time into a huge company that earned billions of dollars. After a while, however, the

FIGURE 3.9 Even if a company isn't paying dividends now, large dividends expected in the future result in a big stock price today.

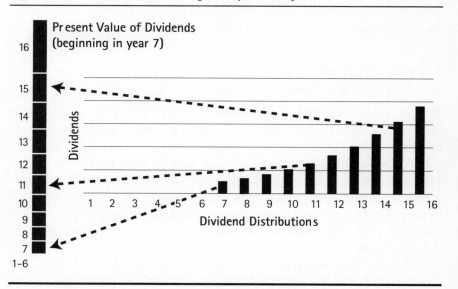

company declined and eventually went bankrupt. Most importantly, suppose that over its entire life it never paid a dividend. If we then flew back to the present and could convince everyone that what we had learned was real and accurate, at that point the price of XYZ company stock should go to zero. I don't care if the company still had 15 years of earnings growth in the billions of dollars ahead of it. Based on our equation for fair price, XYZ's stock price should be zero.

In practice, when dividends lie far in the future, analysts attempt to estimate them by looking at earnings. After all, dividends must eventually come out of earnings. Mature companies often pay out as much as 50% of their earnings as dividends. Therefore, by keeping track of how earnings are growing, analysts can form some idea of what dividends might be in the future.

Today, there are many companies paying few, if any, dividends, as well as many companies doubling and tripling in price that have no earnings at all. If this continues for a long time, investors can start thinking that dividends don't matter. After all, fortunes are being made without any consideration for dividends.

This just shows how fuzzy the numbers can get. The same investors will soon learn the realities of finance if they don't remember that these price movements are 100% speculation. Sooner or later, the price of a stock must have a real basis. Ultimately, the great growth cycle must complete, and the piper must be paid.

Current Dividend Yield and Market Expectation

The fair value term D/I in our model describes the effect of dividends and interest rates on stock prices and helps us understand some important things happening today. One is the current yield on stocks. The current dividend yield on stocks is very low (around 1.3% for the S&P 500). This number is calculated by dividing the current dividend by the current price. What does this low yield mean? To have a low ratio you need to have a high price. From our theory of stacking the money, we know that high prices result from the expectation of very large future dividends (Figure 3.10).

The low dividend yields result because the present dividend is very small compared to the high stack (price) from all those huge expected future dividends. In other words, the current price of stocks is built on a

FIGURE 3.10   The stacking-the-money theory says that a low dividend yield implies that Wall Street is expecting high dividend (and earnings) growth in the future. This expectation of future growth allows investors to accept today's low dividend yield. If confidence in the expected growth were ever shaken, a major price readjustment would occur.

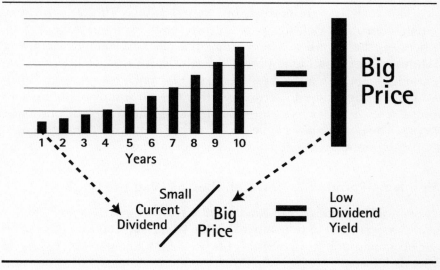

record high expectation of earnings and dividend growth. If this growth doesn't materialize, in hindsight we will know that current prices were too high and the expectations too extreme.

STACKING THE MONEY RESOLVES TWO OF THE INVESTING PARADOXES

We are now in a position to resolve two of the investing paradoxes introduced in Chapter 1.

Resolving Paradox 1: I'm Happy When I'm Sad.

Recall Paradox 1 from Chapter 1: I'm happy when I'm sad. An example of this paradox in action occurred in September 1997, when the government announced the good economic news that payroll levels were increasing. As a result, the stock market sold off 100 points. The press was puzzled to explain it. The analysts said that good news often means that the Fed will raise rates, and this is not good. Carried to its extreme, however, the better the economy gets, the more the market should sell off. Is good news really bad and bad news really good?

The analysts were correct, but they didn't go into the matter in enough detail. In fact, this paradox involves the yin and yang of stock prices explained earlier. After reading this chapter, you now know that interest rates are just as important when calculating stock prices, as are earnings and dividends. Thus, the chain of events makes sense: When employment goes up, investors fear that the government will raise interest rates in order to stem inflation, and higher rates call for lower prices. The positive news indicating that the economy is strengthening is not as important in D/I equations as higher interest rates.

Resolving Paradox 2: How Can the Tail Wag the Dog?

Now recall Paradox 2: How can the tail wag the dog? To understand this paradox, you need to remember that the stock market is one of 12 leading economic indicators, probably the best of the 12. However, to predict the stock market, people usually turn to interest rates. Here is the paradox: The U.S. government classifies interest rates as a lagging economic indicator. Although stocks are one of the first things to move in a business cycle, interest rates are one of the last. How can people use a lagging economic indicator to determine what a leading indicator is about to do? How can the tail wag the dog?

The paradox is resolved when you learn that the word *cycle* comes from the same root as the word *circle*. A rotating point on a circle traces out a normal cycle, or sine wave. Can you find the leading and lagging

FIGURE 3.11 The word *cycle* comes from the same root as the word *circle*. Where is the leading point on a circle, and where is the lagging point?

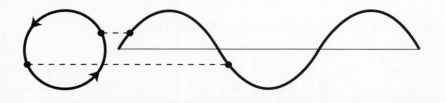

points on the circle in Figure 3.11? It's true that interest rates usually come down at the end of a normal business cycle, but remember that the end of one cycle is the beginning of a new cycle. We should ask why stock prices move up early in the next business cycle. Is it because investors are so good at seeing the higher D (dividends) from an expected new business recovery, or is it because interest rates are lower, making for higher theoretical stock prices? I believe it is because lower rates calculate to higher stock prices.

The theory for fair value indicates that the actual pattern is this: Interest rates come down, signaling the end of the previous business cycle. Lower interest rates allow stock prices, even in the face of deteriorating business, to have a higher fair value, and investors respond. Higher stock prices then seem to indicate the start of the new cycle.

At one time, conventional wisdom held that the stock market was a good leading indicator because investors were farsighted enough to see the new recovery even in the midst of a recession. Early in my career, I couldn't see the end of recessions; I wondered why everyone else had such foresight and I was the one sitting out in the cold. In truth, they weren't clairvoyant; they were just acting according to a theory I had not yet learned: the theory of stacking the money.

4

Technical Analysis and
Unstable Markets

T rying to make money during a trading range market is very difficult. Not only do you have the almost impossible task of locating
the start of such a period (which means, in effect, predicting the
end of a long bull market), you also need to find the beginning and end
of the major swings that will form the trading range.

A long-term bull market, like the one we've been in since 1982,
spoils investors. When prices decline, investors become conditioned to
the idea that if they wait, prices will come back and go higher. They become sloppy because investing becomes too easy—just put your money
in and watch as almost everything moves higher. It's the best of all
worlds. A warning against lazy investing is found in a wise old saying
from market lore: "Never mistake brains for a bull market."

When a long bull market ends and a new period begins, the importance of accurate and disciplined trading again comes to the fore. Stocks
no longer show the characteristic long-term upward advance. Many
stocks decline and never come back. A significant number decline so severely that they wipe out all the gains of the previous long bull market.
At these times, you must have greater trading disciplines and tight guide-
lines that will get you out quickly when your ideas are proved wrong.

Consider Figure 4.1. The dots at the end of the solid line are my projection of the upcoming trend in stock prices. To invest through a period
like this successfully, it is necessary to bring every reliable tool to bear in

FIGURE 4.1   The coming trading range period. The bottom straight line indicates the stock market's long-term trendline since 1928. Notice how the bull market of the last 10 years has pushed prices far away from this trendline. It would be normal for the market to digest these tremendous gains over time by working slowly back and forth until prices end up closer to the line.

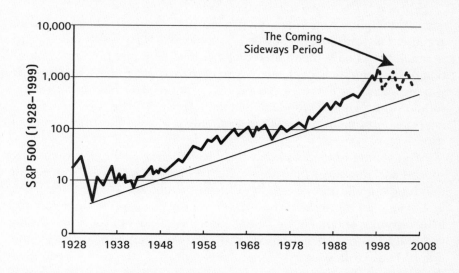

the effort. As I explain in Chapter 6, the Elliott wave pattern is the basic blueprint for forecasting the broad outline of what to expect from prices. However, the trader must always keep every forecast fluid; it is never to be written in concrete. The Elliott wave pattern, with the innumerable and complex variations that the theory allows, by itself is incomplete; you must incorporate other information to help limit the number of possible Elliott wave patterns. One important tool in this effort is technical analysis.

TECHNICAL ANALYSIS VERSUS FUNDAMENTAL ANALYSIS

Two broad studies of the stock market exist: technical analysis and fundamental analysis. In *fundamental analysis*, investors compile and consider economic data in an effort to predict stock prices. They look at sales, earnings, dividends, interest rates, and so forth. In *technical analysis*, investors consider only the information generated on the floor of the exchanges: volume, price history, short interest, put and call ratios, and so on. In fact, you can classify these two disciplines solely by specifying the physical location where the information is generated. If the information originates in the business world, it is fundamental data; if the information originates on the floor of the exchanges, it's technical data.

For years, these two schools have been battling over which one is the correct discipline to predict and explain stock market movements. The argument is quite silly because it is a battle over what really amounts to separate turf. I have mentioned that a clear definition of the time intention of the trade helps determine what type of data you should study. If you are investing for price movements of more than nine months, you should study primarily fundamental data. If you're interested in predicting price movements of less than six months, you should study technical data.

You should understand that technical analysis is the discipline that studies and measures the three feedback-loop terms in the model and that fundamental analysis studies the fair-value term. Because feedback loops can't last more than 3 months maximum in a decline and 6 months in an advance, and major bull and bear markets can last for years, I want to clarify the difference between these two disciplines using a time graph. The clarification takes place as we return to the time intention of the trade.

At the bottom of the graph in Figure 4.2, the X-axis is the time intention of the trade, which is the period of the investment or the period over which you are trying to predict stock prices. It starts with trades lasting a few hours (far left), going into days, weeks, and then months as you move to the right. At the far right are investments that are intended to last a few years. Along the vertical axis, the Y-axis, is a scale that measures

Fundamental analysis is the process of compiling and considering economic data such as sales, earnings, and dividends in an effort to predict stock prices.

Technical analysis is the process of compiling and considering information gathered on the stock exchange floor, such as volume, current stock prices, and short interest, in an effort to predict stock process.

FIGURE 4.2 The relative importance of technical analysis and fundamental analysis in predicting market movement. The time intention of the trade determines which discipline should be used.

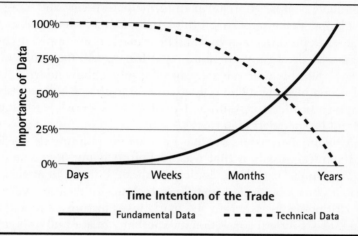

the usefulness of any information to predict, with zero being useless and 100% being vital.

Let's attempt to plot where technical and fundamental analysis fit on this chart. At the far left, where the time intention of the trade is a few days, the importance of technical analysis should be close to 100% and fundamental analysis close to zero. Only technical analysis has any chance of predicting movements lasting a few days. Moving to the right, the situation gradually changes. At the far right, the importance of fundamental analysis is 100% and the importance of technical analysis is zero. Where is the crossover? It's difficult to locate, but I place it somewhere between six and nine months.

CLARIFYING THE TIME LIMITATIONS ON TECHNICAL ANALYSIS

Let's go back to the model of the stock market introduced in Chapter 1. The model holds that stock prices are equal to a fair value stretched and modified by three somewhat independent feedback loops. Now I'm going to make a statement that may surprise, and maybe even upset, some technical analysts. I believe that technical analysis is primarily useful in predicting *only* the price movements caused by the action of the three feedback loops, short-term, intermediate-term, and long-term feedback loops. Because of this, I think that analysts who use only technical analysis to predict major bull and bear markets are applying the discipline incorrectly. In my opinion, any effort to use technical analysis beyond its applicable time range pushes the subject beyond what it is capable of accomplishing. (The only exception to this, I believe, is when high readings in investor sentiment exist simultaneously with extreme levels of public speculation in stocks.)

Many technicians would say that I am wrong, pointing to the deteriorating technical situation that existed before many bear markets as proof that technical signals can anticipate them. I do not deny this. Nevertheless, it is my contention that these technical indicators were incapable of distinguishing whether the market was just unstable and ready for a three-to-six-month correction or whether a major bull or bear market was imminent. In the cases they cite, I believe that the indicators were measuring an instability that eventually transformed itself, for economic reasons, into a lengthy bull or bear market. If a decline is to last more than nine months and turn into a major bear market, there must be an economic reason—a foundation for a decline of this magnitude and time duration.

BASICS OF TECHNICAL ANALYSIS

The Market Technicians Association (MTA) web site (www.MTA-USA.org) lists more than 100 technical indicators of all types. Some 10 or 20 indicators are different types of volume measurement, 20 or 30 measure different periods of the advance-decline line, and so on. You might assume that indicators are measuring many different types of ideas, but there are really only four or five basic ideas in technical analysis. All the various indicators are just different ways to measure these four or five basic concepts.

I can't cover the entire subject of technical analysis in this book, but I will highlight a few of the ideas that are fundamental to the subject. As you read along, keep in mind that there is one additional, and quite important, part of technical analysis not covered in this chapter: the theory of contrary opinion. The theory of contrary opinion is so significant that it has its own chapter (Chapter 5). As you read this chapter, remember that there is an invaluable addition to the technical picture not being described.

Highlighting Divergence

Almost all technical analysis is associated with divergence in one form or another. *Divergence* occurs when two things that were acting together in a certain way start acting separately, or differently, than they did earlier. In technical analysis, unless there is some form of divergence, there is no signal. Almost all the technical tools used, except for the theory of contrary opinion, are based on some type of divergence.

The original Dow theory of the late 1900s was essentially a divergence theory. A hundred years ago, Charles Dow postulated that it is a negative indication when the Dow industrials average goes to new highs but the transportation average fails to follow. This divergence in activity is the basis of the Dow theory. The divergence idea is found throughout technical analysis. If I were to check, I believe I'd find that more than 80% of the indicators at the MTA web site measure some type of divergence.

For example, one of the most basic technical principles, referenced more than any other (except contrary opinion), is when the advance-decline line diverges from the large capitalized indexes. The advance-decline line is the ongoing sum of the number of stocks advancing every day minus the number declining. Usually, this line moves up, along with the various price indexes. At times, however, after a long advance, it makes a top and never again exceeds that point, although the price indexes do. This is the point of divergence. If this divergence continues for a few months, it is a sign of a weak, unstable market.

Many excellent books on technical analysis explain the various indicators and the ideas they are based on. One vital point is seldom covered, however: How do you determine if the technical indicator is signaling strength or weakness over the short, intermediate, or long term? For

---

Divergence is the observation in technical analysis that two indicators or market averages that usually move up and down together are now moving in opposite directions or doing opposite things. One is not confirming the other.

example, how do you determine if the divergence of the advance-decline line is indicating a short-term decline or a long-term one?

An Important Principle: Time Invariance

In 1973, I formulated a principle that has served me well over the years. I call it the principle of time invariance. I have never proved it, I don't know if others have established the same idea or if modern technical works address it, and I have never seen it stated in the books I've read. It is a principle very similar to the concept behind fractals (covered in Chapter 6). The principle is this: *In technical analysis, what is true for the long term is true for the short term.*

The Principle of Time Invariance

In technical analysis, what is true for the long term is true for the short term. What this means is that if some technical principle is discovered that applies to intermediate-term movements, the same principle will be found to apply to short-term moves—only the time scale changes.

What this principle means is that, in technical analysis, if there is a certain sequence of events that usually occurs at a major market top or bottom, you'll find the same sequence, albeit smaller in size, before a short-term market top or bottom. For example, in a bull market, total market volume usually peaks before stock prices reach their peak, generally about four months before. You will find volume also peaks before price in a move that lasts only four weeks. In this case, however, it peaks maybe five or six days before the price peaks. Everything is scaled back in terms of time, but the sequence is the same.

The model we have put forth is that stock prices equal a fair value modified and stretched by three feedback loops. Each feedback loop can cause exaggerated price movements in its time realm. If you are attempting to predict prices over the very short term, you use the same technical tools scaled to the time scale. In other words, you don't need different technical tools to predict different-size moves—you just scale back the time frame of the tool.

For example, when measuring volume, a very short-term trader might go to a moving average of hourly volumes to compare. An intermediate-term trader might use a moving average of daily volume, and a longer-term investor might use weekly volume. What this principle says is that, no matter the time scale, each would look for the same pattern or divergence over that time scale.

In my opinion, not knowing or misunderstanding this principle is the cause of some of the misstatements made by market technicians. They get confused about the time frame referenced by the technical indicator they are looking at. This is also true when comparing the different characteristics between market tops and market bottoms. The technical differences one finds between long-term tops and long-term bottoms are the same differences that distinguish short-term tops and bottoms.

The Two Categories of Technical Indicators

We can classify technical indicators into two types. I call the first type a transition indicator and the second, a confirming indicator. The first indicator tries to locate exact market tops and bottoms—transition points where the market is changing trend. The other indicator type doesn't look for market tops or bottoms but defines when a market trend has been established, confirming when a new trend is in play. Confirming indicators give signals after a top or bottom has been made. The idea behind it is to let the market make top or bottom, then get in afterward and ride the trend.

You can appropriately classify indicators as one or the other: Does it mark a transition point (a top or bottom) or does it respond after a top or bottom, confirming a market that has established a trend? Remember that these two approaches always conflict. A transition indicator such as contrary opinion always looks best at the worst point in the trend of the market. Keep them separate in your mind; their goals and targets are completely different.

Understanding the Difference between
Market Tops and Bottoms

From a technical perspective, market tops and bottoms behave differently, and you use different technical tools for each. Tops are usually long, large, rounded affairs (think of an open fan), often to the point where it becomes difficult to find the exact top. The top seems to be spread out, and it appears to be more of a process than an event. Bottoms are different. Bottoms are usually short, they end quickly, and they are rather easy to locate. They are more of an event than a process (Figure 4.3).

It's important to realize that these are just the *usual* forms of tops and bottoms; otherwise, you may not recognize something because a fixed idea prevents you from considering it. This happened to many analysts in 1982. The 1982 bear-market bottom was not a normal event bottom. The bottom didn't occur suddenly on a single day but stretched over six months as a rolling, compression bottom. In Figure 4.4, you can see the compression process in the contracting number of stocks that made new lows as the market worked lower. I started to see the evidence for what was happening in the late spring of 1982, about three months before the final bottom. When I spotted what was happening, watching the market finish the process and make bottom was like watching a three-act play: The bottom occurred in the final act. Holding to the idea that declines end only in climaxes prevented many technicians from seeing that this was a process bottom and not an event bottom, even though the evidence was there.

FIGURE 4.3   Market bottoms are usually abrupt and end quickly. Market tops usually form over an extended period.

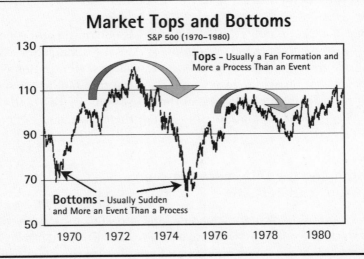

FIGURE 4.4 The unusual 1982 "process bottom." The top line plots the number of stocks making new lows. While the New York composite index went lower, the decreasing number of stocks hitting new lows pointed to the compression process in progress. Careful study of individual stocks shows that hundreds of them went through powerful "saucer bottoms" as the process continued. (Source: © DecisionPoint.com.)

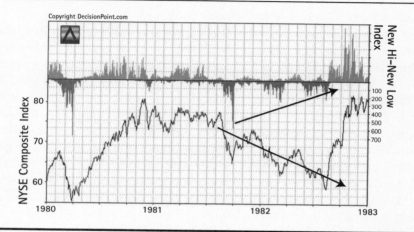

In technical analysis, the underlying idea is that in any bull market or major price movement, there is a normal sequence of events that takes place internally in the market as the topping process occurs. What do I mean by *internally*? In Chapter 1, I discussed the analogy of statistical mechanics in physics with the movement of many stocks in the stock market. It is easier to predict the whole stock market than to predict any individual stock, just as it is easier to predict the overall movement of all the gas molecules than the movement of any individual molecule. By *internal market*, I mean looking at and categorizing statistically what the individual stocks are doing that make up the whole market.

Internal market consists of the statistical measurements, such as the number of stocks making new highs or lows and the number of advancing stocks versus decliners, that describe what is happening to the mass of individual stocks as the overall market moves up or down.

To understand this, remember that the market is the average of all stocks. The S&P 500, for example, is the average of the price activity of the 500 largest stocks. Everything is summarized by one simple number, but it is a one-dimensional view. When the S&P 500 is up, it doesn't mean that all 500 stocks are up; it means only that a mathematical average of the 500 is up. But there are a large variety of different internal markets that can calculate to the same number.

Let me clarify this. Suppose that on two consecutive days, the S&P 500 is up 1%. From this one number both days look the same. If we went a little deeper and statistically measured what the individual components were doing, we might see a different picture. Maybe on one day, only 20 of the 500 stocks are up, but those 20 are up a lot, and the other 480 stocks are down but down just a bit. On the second day, all 500 stocks are up, but they all are up just a little bit. Both days produce the same 1% mathematical average gain and look the same on the outside, but an internal look presents a completely different picture. Therefore, technicians are always looking inside the market, at the market internals.

They look at how many stocks are making new highs and new lows as the major market indexes are advancing. They also look at the number of stock advancing versus those that are declining. They are looking for divergences. For example, it is not a good sign to see more stocks hitting new lows than new highs while the major indices are hitting all-time highs. Similarly, it's not a good sign to see total volume contracting while prices are breaking to new highs.

Recognizing a Normal Market Cycle

What occurs internally in a normal market cycle? Usually, at the start of a major advance, most stocks move up together. The pattern continues for some time. This is good, and it's the way it should be.

This pattern is measured by market breadth. *Market breadth* measures the number of stocks advancing each day versus the number declining. It doesn't matter how much a stock has advanced or declined; a 1/8th-point advance is just as important as a 10-point advance. Any stock that advances at all is an advancing stock. If the market averages are going up, technicians like to see good breadth, in which the number of stocks advancing is a large number, not a small number.

History teaches us something. Usually, as a stock market advance matures, the averages continue to go up, but fewer stocks participate, which means that investors are starting to narrow their focus. A few stocks are going up a lot while many other stocks are languishing or declining a little. This is not good.

The volume of trading also stops expanding and actually starts to shrink as the averages move to their final highs. Normally in the beginning of a move, the volume of trading continually grows. At a certain point, the market makes new highs, but the volume contracts. This sets up a divergence between volume and price.

The Perfect Indicator?

Investors and technicians often search through countless investing books looking for the one indicator that reliably predicts the market. Although this can be very instructive, heed my admonition: When you evaluate all the technical indicators, don't lose track of the general concept on which each indicator is based. Those concepts are the important points. If you pay too much attention to the fine details and the intricate wiggles of some indicator, you often lose sight of the big picture. Any indicator is just there to help you see the larger story the market is telling; don't give that indicator some magical importance beyond that. Indicators are just tools to help you see what is happening in various segments and sectors of the market.

After searching for more than 30 years, I have learned that there isn't a perfect indicator. You will not find it. But there is also a weakness in searching through all the indicators and something to warn you about.

Remember that the market is, more often than not, unpredictable. During these long unpredictable periods, investors and technicians often become frantic trying to figure it out. They investigate all the indicators looking for some subtle clue. They often start stretching things and magnifying subtle unimportant indications out of proportion trying to find the answer. However, the market at that moment is simply saying it is unpredictable. Don't push it.

Be careful—this is a major trap. At those moments, it is best to back away and say, "I don't know," and then wait until the picture becomes clear and conclusive. Before every major move, the market will tell you very clearly what is happening. The indication is never some subtle obscure wiggle in an indicator. When it happens, you'll see it.

Divergence is a sign that the topping process has begun. Recall that market tops are usually large, rounded, fan formations and are more a process than an event. Different stocks and different stock groups usually top at different times. Various market divergences are a sign that this is occurring. The problem is that the process can take some time; there is no way of knowing how long the process will take—it could take two months or two years. It is common to take a bearish posture two or three times before the real decline begins.

Making Top

As I stated before, in the process of the market topping, certain events usually happen before the general averages make top (Figure 4.5). First, as the bull market matures, the number of stocks making new highs hits a peak number. In other words, even though the market averages are going up and continuing to make new highs, the actual number of stocks making new highs does not increase.

FIGURE 4.5 The normal sequence of indicator divergences as the market goes into the topping process. (A–D line = advance-decline line.)

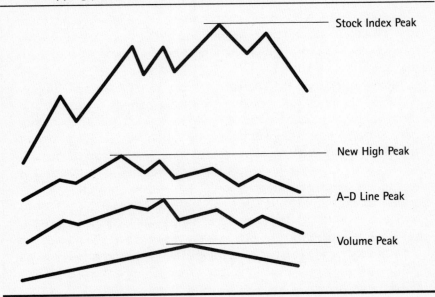

Second, as the popular averages continue to new highs, the *advance-decline line*, which is the difference between the number of stocks advancing and the number declining, fails to confirm (i.e., it fails to make a new high). This sets up the popular technical indication of the divergence between the advance-decline line and the popular averages.

Finally, the daily trading volume fails to expand, which sets up the third divergence. As a bull market continues, the volume of trading usually grows. At a certain point, prices continue to new highs, but the volume of trading stops growing and actually contracts. This can happen for a little while without cause for worry, but if it continues, it is usually the final important indication that the topping process is just about complete. Thus the long-held observation that price follows volume.

Where is the top? It is spread out over time and has been occurring all along at different points for different stocks. Many stocks made their highs around the time the number of new highs peaked. Other stocks made their highs when the advance-decline line made its high. Still others will make their highs *after* the averages have peaked. The action of various stock groups topping at different points in time is the fan formation, the topping process I referred to earlier. It is important to note that the process *usually* goes this way, but there are so many variations that the variations are really the rule.

Topping Often Starts in Wave Four

From my experience through many markets, the process of topping often starts in the fourth wave of the Elliott wave movement, especially if it is a complex horizontal movement. (In Chapter 6, you will learn more about the Elliott wave.) For now, let's just say that any major advance takes place in three thrusts separated by two pullbacks. The thrusting waves are labeled waves one, three, and five; the separating pullbacks are waves two and four. You can see this basic pattern in Figure 4.6.

Sometimes, if the first two advancing waves are big and of long duration, the second correction, wave four, is often long and very complex. When wave four is protracted and complex, the divergences mentioned often start at the top of wave three, not the top of wave five, which is the actual top in the major indexes. If this happens, the divergence lasts a long time before the wave five top.

This event is the cause of more prognostication errors by market technicians than any other. I've seen it so often that I have come to look for it as a market indicator itself. Here is what happens: As the market

FIGURE 4.6   After a long advance, there is often an extended fourth-wave correction before the final fifth wave to new highs. Market divergences often start during this wave four, indicating that many stocks peaked at the top of wave three and will not make new highs when the final, fifth wave occurs. It is common for some market technicians, seeing the divergences, to become bearish too soon and get confused when the market breaks to new highs.

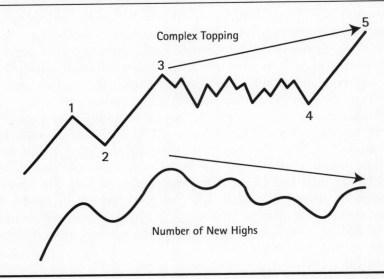

moves into a complex wave four, it gives the appearance of starting to round over. Remember, a complex wave four usually occurs after strong waves one and three, with a short wave two correction separating them. Some people start getting nervous after this big run-up and are ready for a reaction. They begin noticing the technical divergences as the corrective wave four forms. At this point, technicians often call the top.

As the market moves sideways, forming wave four, more and more people start taking a bearish stance, expecting the market to break. Every little decline during the complex wave four raises hopes that this is the beginning of the widely anticipated decline and, although the market looks weak, each decline unexpectedly halts, and the market recovers a little.

The market then slowly advances to the previous peaks but looks very weak. Volume is low. Suddenly prices break to new highs and a strong rally begins. The final wave five has started. For a short period, the advance-decline line again comes back to life, looking strong, and technical factors seem to be in gear. At this point, the majority of analysts quickly swing back to the bullish view, often saying the divergences were a false signal. They weren't; they were just a little early. It is at this point, as investors and analysts swings back to the bullish side, that you should start getting very bearish.

Now psychology enters the picture. Many investors will be found to have locked themselves out psychologically. After being bearish for some time and then admitting an error and changing back to being bullish, they are now very reluctant to flip-flop and become bearish even if prices start into a decline. They are afraid to take a bearish stance again. As prices start to decline—in other words, prices do what people originally thought they would do—these people are somewhat frozen in a bullish posture by their reluctance to reverse position.

One of the most important lessons the trader has to learn is being able to flip-flop in opinion when it is actually called for. You have to be willing to admit you were wrong. This is an example of how you can basically be right about the market, but you are right too early, which can spoil everything. Survival in the market is often simply the effort to maintain confidence in your own judgment.

Making Bottom

Market bottoms are different from market tops from a technical viewpoint. Very few technical indicators, except market sentiment, are useful at calling a bottom. Unless it's a very rare compression bottom (as in 1982), most bottoms end in some form of a climax. A *climax* is a type of market bottom in which panic selling occurs in huge volumes, with prices collapsing completely. The climax actually starts days earlier, and as the decline continues, the volume in stocks rise as prices plummet, until it becomes a panic.

The actual end, or bottom, usually occurs in one day. What happens is that prices collapse on huge volume, and then, mid-trading day, reverse direction and surge upward, also on huge volume. This reversal rally dies away after a few days, after which prices go into a long, quiet period during which nothing much happens and volume becomes extremely light. The market looks dead, which it is, but the decline is over.

During a selling climax, it's best not to look for the bottom. Take a step back, or, if you are invested and think it's early enough, sell out and repurchase later. Let the market make climactic bottom and go through its reversal rally.

When the reversal rally is over, it almost always declines again by at least 50% or more of the rally. On this pullback, the volume usually dries up to almost nothing; it's the death after the climax. At this moment, the market seems awfully weak, and there doesn't seem to be any reason for it to go up anytime soon. Investor sentiment measures are extremely negative; investors are generally expecting further price declines. The most optimistic talk is that the market will need a lot of confidence building before anything positive happens. You've got your opportunity! At this point, it is usually safe to purchase for the long term—and you won't have to wait for as long as you may think!

Changing Market Patterns

Many possible market patterns can occur. Some of the important ones have already been listed in books on technical analysis. The market often sets a particular pattern that continues to recur. If you are lucky, you can often profit from them. They are best kept to yourself because if widely broadcast, the pattern tends to disappear.

For example, suppose you notice that for the last three short-term market thrusts, the Dow Jones industrial averages rose sharply, but for the first three days of each move, the NASDAQ stayed relatively flat. On the fourth day, the NASDAQ played catch-up, rising very dramatically. The NASDAQ doesn't normally do this; it is something you have just noticed recently. Maybe speculators have become much more cautious than normal and hold back, waiting for the move to be real before they go into the NASDAQ-type stocks. Use that observation. Maybe it isn't real but it probably is; try it out at the next opportunity.

An intermediate-term trader, noticing this pattern for short-term moves, further notices that the market has begun what looks like a longer-term move. She notices also that the move is primarily a Dow Jones industrials move again, with the NASDAQ holding back. She can conclude one of two things: This move will continue (strong Dow, weak NASDAQ) or it is a manifestation over the longer term of a pattern seen previously in short-term moves. I'd assume the second and take a position based on that assumption. One reason to do this is that such situations allow a trader to know when she or he is wrong with the least amount of risk.

Many of these patterns are real and can be used to make money. They originate for some reason that doesn't have to be known, they exist for a time, then often fade away. Make these observations your own. You will find that once you have a correct operating model for stock prices, you will be able to see and understand them better. It will help increase your confidence that your model is indeed correct.

Let me give you an example. By December of 2000, the market had just gone through a severe four-month decline. Most of the selling had been in the NASDAQ. The NASDAQ-type stocks kept going down, day after day with no let up into the last week of the year, but the volume was getting low. It seemed that, after four months, the continued selling was primarily tax selling. More and more people who were waiting for a rally to take their tax loss gave up each day as no rally materialized. In other words, the current selling was almost 100% done to realize a loss to be used against any gains taken earlier in the year.

I figured the tax selling would continue right to the end of the year. Then the selling would suddenly lift. So on the last day of the year, I bought some QQQ and some HHH; these are exchange-traded funds of NASDAQ and Internet stocks, respectively. I figured there would be a very sudden lifting of the tax selling in these sectors and, with help from short sellers covering their positions, these stocks would literally be sucked upward in price, as in a vacuum. They would go up not because of heavy buying but simple lack of selling.

On the first day of trading in the year 2001, January 2, the market continued down. Both QQQ and HHH declined. The next day, things changed dramatically: A huge advance was led by both QQQ and HHH, each making double-digit percentage gains in one day. Suddenly the QQQ was up more than 7% from the end of December and the HHH up more than 10%. That was it—the market sagged off and the move was over for a few days. It was a nice profit. You'll find that these moments, in which you see something and then act on it and it proves out, are the most satisfying ones.

The Pivotal Point

The pivotal point has long been discussed with regard to technical analysis. Jesse Livermore's book *How to Trade in Stocks*, has an entire chapter about the pivotal point. He begins by saying, "Whenever I have had the patience to wait for the market to arrive at what I call a 'Pivotal Point' before I started to trade, I have always made money in my operations." The problem is that he never really defines what he means by a pivotal point.

Essentially, a pivotal point is a price or a moment in time from which you'll know real soon which way the market will go. (For more about Livermore, see the sidebar about him on page 47). The trouble is that a pivotal point for me is not a pivotal point for someone else. The location of the point depends on the model one is using to understand the market.

The breaking of a trendline on a price chart is an example of by a pivotal point: It represents a clear cutoff where the trend of the market has been broken or a new trend started. The reason a pivotal point is so valuable is that it allows a trader to know when a trade is wrong with the least amount of loss. This is especially true if the trade is longer term. Suppose the market moves up and threatens to break above a long-term declining trendline. It then breaks through and moves up on expanding volume. The investor takes a position. The odds are that the market might pull back, but if it is the real thing, it should not break below the line again. If it does, one should then sell out with a small loss. If it does carry through as expected, one has entered into a long-term trade at a very favorable starting point, and done it with very little risk.

If the market fails and the loss is taken, the investor might feel bad about the loss. I don't. I understand that here was an opportunity to make a large gain, and I tested the waters with minimal loss. This time it was a loss; the next time probably won't be. Remember that any trade is only one trade in what will amount to a thousand over time. Don't ever put everything, either mentally or emotionally, into a single trade.

I have observed something about pivotal points on and off for many years. It is this: At times the stock market can become very indecisive. Volatility dies down, and the market seems to lack direction. As this continues, more and more people start noticing the lack of direction. This lack of direction will usually manifest in all three time domains, short, intermediate, and long term.

When that happens, you start noticing that everyone, and I mean everyone, starts looking at shorter and shorter price moves to resolve the indecision, or they look with a microscope at an impending news item to resolve the uncertainty. When an announcement comes in, the response is normally huge, as investors take the result as a resolution of the indecision. It seldom is. Beware when it seems that all of Wall Street is looking at one short-term event or one news item to tell them what is going to happen long term. These widely agreed-to pivotal points are seldom the real ones.

Unstable Markets

Unstable markets, in which feedback loops are on the verge of being triggered, usually have the common characteristic of a lack of volatility right before the triggering. In my experience, the following occurs: The market will have advanced to a new high and seem to be holding that position very well. Sell-offs, when they occur, are moderate and don't seem to amount to anything. These weak sell-offs often induce people to observe how strong the market looks after the recent advance; they say that it doesn't seem like it wants to go down. Slowly, the market becomes very calm, then it gradually moves to new highs on very light volume. Prices often seem to go right out on a ledge, slowly rolling over and picking up steam as trading volume rises. The decline often catches people off guard. The stock market has lulled investors into complacency. These declines start with low volatility, often becoming very severe in terms of price, and end with high volatility.

The best indication of an unstable market ready to be triggered is the following: low volatility, low volume and either extreme bullish or bearish investor sentiment. (You will see the importance of sentiment in the next chapter, which is on the theory of contrary opinion.) It is normal to have extreme bearish sentiment as the market goes into a steep decline with high volatility. If the market quiets down, however, and the bearish sentiment is still very high while volume is very low, you have a situation that is actually very unstable, and a major move to the upside is imminent (a positive feedback). Likewise, it is normal to have high bullish sentiment as prices roar forward and hit new highs. However, when prices quiet down at a high price level while volume dries up and sentiment stays extremely bullish—watch out. That is a very weak market.

Obscuring the Obvious

Probably more than half of the technical market indicators are oscillators of one kind or another. I find oscillators far overrated. Twenty-five years ago, I used and tested hundreds of them; now I never use them. I stopped because I found that they are a form of esoteric mathematics that often prevent a person from seeing what is happening. Using them often encourages a person to put something more into the market than is really there—a major weakness that I warned about earlier. I follow the wisdom of a famous physicist: "Don't fall in love with beautiful math." If you can't see what is happening in the market, you won't discover a deeper truth by studying an oscillator; it can't tell you anything more than the original statistic on which the oscillator is based.

I know I'm being overly critical here, but I'm trying to make a point. For example, many oscillators are calculated from the advance-decline line. The advance-decline line is simply the difference between two numbers: the number of stocks advancing and the number declining. There is no greater truth buried in this number. The creation of the advance decline line was originally intended simply to pinpoint market divergences, periods when the popular averages were going up while most stocks were going down. That's all. Then people started taking moving averages of the line. They began subtracting one moving average from another moving average and plotting this line. They started adding these differences and plotting the sum. They even started looking for trendlines of this measure.

You can see how this process can slowly remove a person from a simple and direct observation of the market. Doing this is a little like taking a simple equation, such as $1 + 1 = 2$, squaring it, taking the fifth root, and then adding 3 to it. Doing more to this number won't give you any greater truth than the original simple equation of $1 + 1 = 2$. It is unnecessary mathematical complexity to find some deep meaning underneath all the data, but there isn't any. That is not the direction to proceed to discover what the stock market is going to do.

Just by looking at the advance-decline line, I can tell you what any oscillator will look like. The oscillators are calculated from the advance-decline line, so they can't tell you anything that the line itself can't tell you. With many oscillators, technical analysts are simply bottling up tap water, adding bells, whistles, and a little mystery, and selling it as a magical potion. It's just plain tap water.

Computers as Traders

I'm expecting that a new investing rage will emerge after the market has been in a trading range for some time: computer programs that do all the trading for us. These programs will monitor the financial markets 24 hours a day, automatically call up an Internet account, and make the trades when and as they see fit. If a computer can now beat the world chess champion, a computer that can consistently do better than the best human trader is not far off.

When a trading range market sets up and becomes accepted as the new investment reality and when trading programs start producing consistently better returns than their human counterparts, the movement toward this type of computer program will quicken. Humans will just stand back and watch, much like they now do at the computer chess tournaments. I think this could happen by the year 2005.

PARADOX 3 RESOLVED

We are now in a position to resolve Paradox 3 of the investing paradoxes presented in the Introduction.

Paradox 3: The technician says up and the fundamentalist says down—yet both are right. The fundamental analyst, after looking at the economic situation, proclaims that all is well and says that stocks will advance. The technician, after studying new highs and lows, the advance-decline line, and price patterns says that the stock market will decline. Both are right. How can this be?

Both analysts can be correct because they are referring to—or should be referring to—different time frames. It is unfortunate that this point is seldom clarified, not clarifying it is the cause of half of the seemingly contradictory advice you hear from analysts.

5

Of BABES, O'BUCS, and Contrary Opinion

The theory of contrary opinion is a trader's most important decision-making tool. Whenever I'm away from the market for any length of time, the first thing I check when I get back are my contrary opinion indicators. Many investors and analysts consider contrary opinion important but, in my opinion, not important enough. Most of them have trouble applying it correctly.

To successfully navigate the trading range market that I believe we have entered, contrary opinion will at times be the only guide pointing to the correct course of action. To apply contrary opinion successfully, we must understand why people have trouble using it. The primary reason investors have trouble applying the theory is because they have to reject the obviously correct story that is making everyone so bearish or bullish. This difficulty is explained by what I call BABES and O'BUCS.

THE THEORY OF CONTRARY OPINION

In March 1972, the well-known market analyst, Marty Zweig, wrote an article for *Barron's* called "The Dearth of Short Selling." In it, he predicted a stock market decline, arguing that the lack of short selling indicated too much investor optimism. (Short selling is a way to make money if stocks decline. The extreme lack of it means investors are very optimistic about higher prices.) That March was the month when the majority of stocks hit their peak, and nine months later, the popular averages began their greatest decline of our generation, producing the two-year bear market (1973 to 1974).

Two and a half years later, with the market at the bottom, a brash 29-year-old market student (me) walked into his broker's office and declared that the current market represented the "buy of the decade." Because my broker's business had declined so severely, my declaration seemed like a grim joke; in fact, it almost got me thrown out of the room! Even though I believed what I said and was ultimately right, it felt very strange saying the words, like coming in after a devastating tornado and enthusiastically declaring, "Aren't we going to have fun rebuilding everything from scratch!"

What gave me the courage to say something so outrageous? I was looking at the same short-selling indicator that Marty Zweig had highlighted two years earlier. This time, however, it was indicating the opposite situation—it was showing one of the highest levels of short selling in history, reflecting pessimism so deep that it just had to be a major market bottom. Such is the power of the theory of contrary opinion.

What Is the Theory?

The theory of contrary opinion is very simple: When the vast majority of market participants think stock prices will advance, they usually decline. Likewise, when the vast majority thinks prices will decline, they advance. In other words, prices will move contrary to what investors expect when those expectations have reached an extreme. I want to emphasize the last point: The theory applies only when those expectations have reached an extreme. Notice that the theory does not consider the general economic situation. It simply states that the *necessary and sufficient condition for a major market top or bottom is the existence of extreme bullish or bearish sentiment*. That's quite a statement.

The *theory of contrary opinion* states that when the vast majority of market participants think stock prices will advance, they usually decline. When the vast majority thinks prices will decline, they usually advance. The importance and truth of the theory is best summarized by the statement: the necessary and sufficient condition to signal the start of a major movement up or down in stock prices is extreme investor sentiment.

Both history and experience have shown me that an investor's best chance of success at predicting stock prices is the theory of contrary opinion. When you have an extreme reading in market sentiment, you must elevate that fact above all other indicators and economic data. It doesn't mean that these other indicators aren't important, it just means that when they conflict with an extreme reading in sentiment, you always defer to contrary opinion. When you make this mental adjustment, however, it forces you into an interesting inversion of thinking that I call BABES and O'BUCS.

BABES and O'BUCS

If contrary opinion is a fundamental theory in predicting stock prices, as I and many others say, then it follows that there must be a BABES and an O'BUCS. *BABES* is my acronym for a *b*roadly *a*greed to *b*ut *e*ssentially wrong *s*cenario. *O'BUCS* stands for *o*ccluded *b*ut *u*ltimately *c*orrect *s*cenario. The basic idea is that, at moments of extreme readings of investor sentiment, the obvious economic explanation behind that expectation must be wrong—there must be some holes in the data or thinking about the data. Thus, in applying the theory of contrary opinion, you use it to direct your attention to discovering the true and correct economic scenario—finding the O'BUCS idea. *Locating the* O'BUCS *idea is the action of finding today the economic explanation that will emerge in the future to explain why stock prices moved opposite to what everyone expected.*

These concepts about BABES and O'BUCS evolved during my reading of *Barron's* magazine for 30 years, but I also give credit to Alan Abelson and his ideas in *Up and Down Wall Street*. As a contrarian, Abelson

---

BABES *Broadly Agreed to But Essentially wrong Scenario.* The economic reason, or story, that has been constructed to explain why the stock market will do what the majority of investors expect it to do. It is the economic *why* that supports the extreme bullish or bearish feeling.

O'BUCS *Occluded But Ultimately Correct Scenario.* The obscured or hidden economic reason that will emerge in the future to explain why stock prices went in the opposite direction to what everyone thought.

would often point to an indicator that showed enormous investor optimism and then discuss, with that wonderful sardonic humor, what the majority view was probably missing.

I learned another lesson from reading all those *Barron's* stories—I learned to be very cautious. *Barron's* often revisits an investment after it fails or goes bankrupt to review why it failed. This allowed me to learn the various ways investors can miss things: I came to see that when everyone agrees that a particular idea is valid, you should look very intently in the other direction to identify the holes in their thinking.

The major hurdle is that to apply the theory of contrary opinion you must overcome the fundamental ideas that are making everyone so bullish or bearish. If the picture of the economy looks extremely good, no clouds are in sight, and everyone is bullish, the fact that everyone is bullish becomes more important than anything else. I came to have confidence that the world worked in this strange kind of way. My first book, written in late 1999, was really just an application of the basic ideas of BABES and O'BUCS to the market in 1999.

Understanding Why the Theory of Contrary Opinion Works

After 30 years of study and application, the theory of contrary opinion still mystifies me; I don't completely understand why it works. No one has ever explained it to my satisfaction. To me it is a little like the quantum theory—physicists use it and talk about it, but does anyone really understand it? Nothing I've read or heard completely explains the accuracy of the theory of contrary opinion. Nevertheless, the fact that top-flight market analysts, such as Marty Zweig, Bernie Schaeffer, Robert Farrell, and others, have made major prognostications based solely on this one theory shows how powerful many people consider it.

For one thing, contrary opinion seems to explain why it's so difficult to make money in the stock market. If markets simply went in the direction the majority thought they would, making money would be easy and we'd all be rich. I think it was the observable fact that this isn't the case, combined with the high correlation between extremes in sentiment with market tops and bottoms, that originally convinced me of the value of this theory.

The usual explanation of why the theory of contrary opinion works is based on this simple idea: If everyone is bullish, the majority of investors have already made their purchases, which means there is no one left to buy and there is no means of driving prices higher. In the same vein, if everyone is bearish, most people have probably already sold their stocks, meaning that no one has any stocks left to sell.

It is a good explanation, but it doesn't account for everything. For example, I have seen markets that went through a small sideways correction after a big advance and ended with extremely bearish readings— readings equal to those you see at major bear market bottoms. Yet the number of possible sellers after such a small correction couldn't possibly have been exhausted—not like at the end of a bear market. Until we get a better explanation for the theory of contrary opinion, however, this one will suffice.

A Brief History of the Theory

Contrary opinion as a theory was first defined in 1954 by Humphrey Neill in his book, *The Art of Contrary Thinking*, but I'm sure it was known further back than that. The basic concept can be found in a number of earlier works.

For example, in Edwin Lefevre's book, *Reminiscences of a Stock Operator,* written in 1917, there is the statement, "Always buy when complete demoralization has set in." In 1939, Charles Hardy did an extensive study called "Odd-Lot Trading on the New York Exchange." It seems to be the first effort to see how the small investor's buying and selling compares to market performance. Later, Garfield A. Drew took that data and, in *New Methods for Profit in the Stock Market*, pioneered what became known as the odd lot theory. According to this theory, the small investor, being the least sophisticated investor of the investor classes, ends up buying more at a market top and selling more at a market bottom.

From these ideas emerged a number of other efforts based on trying to measure what investors were doing. In the1940s, both the New York Stock Exchange (NYSE) and the Securities and Exchange Commission (SEC) began publishing information about the buying, selling, and short selling of other investor groups. These efforts gave rise to various technical indicators, such as the short interest ratio and the NYSE credit-debit balance. Then Humphrey Neill pulled all these efforts together under one unifying theory called contrary opinion.

As we study this evolution through the 1940s and 1950s, we start noticing that two distinct but related ideas emerge. One is the idea of applying the theory by measuring the percentage of bullishness or bearishness in a group of investors. The other idea is to measure how big that group of investors is or how big a certain investor activity has become. The distinction here should be clearly understood.

It is a little like observing a crowd assembling below you for a political rally, Democrats on one side and Republicans on the other. There are two things you could measure. One is the comparative size of the two sides (for example, twice as many Democrats as Republicans). The second is measuring the total size of the crowd, irrespective of affiliation, which would indicate the degree of interest in the subject matter of the rally.

It is important to separate these two distinct but related concepts: measuring the percent of bullishness or bearishness and measuring the breadth of investor interest. For example, in 1978, after 13 years of dismal stock returns, only 16% of the American public held stocks. Interest in stock investing was at an all-time low. During this period on September 29, 1978, however, investor sentiment gave a high bullish reading. The market had rallied for 6 months, and bullish sentiment, *for those who were investing*, was extremely intense. Therefore, sentiment was very bullish for those interested in stock investing although the *level of interest* in stocks was low. By 1999, the situation had changed. In January 1999, the same indicator of investor sentiment was giving the same reading as it did in 1978. However, now 60% of the American public, after a 17-year bull market, had been lured back into stocks, showing high public interest in stock investing.

When analysts talk of sentiment, they are usually referring to the comparative bullishness or bearishness of those investing. When they talk about the intensity of public involvement in stocks or the fervor behind it, they usually call these speculation indices.

It is important to distinguish these two concepts. All bull markets always end with the investing participants bullish, but all great bull markets end with *broad public interest* in stock investing. It is a long-accepted concept that great bull markets end when everyone is playing the stock investing game, talking about it at cocktail parties and over back yard fences.

Since its formative years, the theory of contrary opinion has changed little. What has changed, however, are the methods analysts use to determine what investors are feeling at the moment. Many former indicators that worked very well have been made useless by the new derivative investments. Some still work well.

Is Investor Sophistication a Factor?

One of the oldest ideas about stock investing is that investors can be classified into categories and ranked by their investment knowledge and sophistication. There are people in the know and those on the outside (insiders versus outsiders). The concept is that sophisticated investors would be relatively right about the market, and the uninformed investor would be relatively wrong.

The odd lot theory developed in the 1930s was an attempt to describe the class of investor that is usually wrong at market turning points. There have been attempts to try to locate the other side—the groups that show correct market activity at turning points. I have never been satisfied with the results.

Significantly, Humphrey Neill's formulation of contrary opinion in 1954 doesn't distinguish whose opinion we are measuring. It says only that at major market junctures the widely accepted opinion about market direction will be wrong. After searching for years, I have come to the conclusion that almost any large body of individuals, no matter their level of sophistication, generally holds the wrong opinion at critical market junctures. In other words, there is no class of investors whose investment actions are usually right at major turning points.

This seems to be true of mutual fund money managers as a group. You would think that this would be a sophisticated group, yet according to statistics, they usually have the highest cash position in the funds they manage at a market bottom (when they should be fully invested) and the least amount at the top (when they should have lots of cash). Some people attribute this to investor redemption, but a careful study disproves it.

Similarly, it was commonly believed that the trading activity of Wall Street firms and floor specialists showed that they were indeed very sophisticated and usually right with their investments. Statistics of their trading activity seemed to confirm it. In my opinion, however, the calculation wasn't measuring what everyone thought it was. Other measurements often showed a different picture.

With that said, the only group that did seem to be somewhat right with their investments were corporate insiders—the corporate officers and directors who have to register with the SEC when they want to buy or sell their companies' stocks. Their buying and selling generally seemed to turn out pretty well, but outside of this small group, I have found no others.

HOW INVESTOR EXPECTATIONS ARE MEASURED

The methods for measuring investor expectations fall into two categories. The first attempts to measure what investors are thinking by calculating ratios based on what they are doing—their transactions. The second category measures what investors are thinking by directly polling them to assess their opinions on the market.

It's important to note that no matter which method you use (measuring investment activity or polling), the data is applied in the same way. In practice, you must have a fair amount of data on hand, enough to back-test the data through a number of severe bull and bear markets. You need long historical data to determine with any accuracy what levels represent extreme investor sentiment for that indicator. For example, if some indicator or ratio goes to a reading of two at four separate bear market bottoms, you set two as an extreme reading of bearish sentiment for that indicator.

First Method: Investor Activity

Investor activity can be measured by looking at a variety of indicators, including short-selling ratios, put/call ratios, the volatility index, and the Rydex ratio.

The Short-Selling Ratios

An investor usually sells stock short when he or she is expecting a decline. Thus, the amount of short selling in the market is usually a measure of bearish sentiment. In the past, analysts have measured short selling in a variety of ways: odd-lot short selling, total public short selling, member short selling, specialist short selling, and short open interest. For example, Figure 5.1 shows the specialist short-selling ratio from

FIGURE 5.1   This chart plots the famous specialist's short-selling indicator, which is similar to the short-selling indicator Marty Zweig used in his 1972 *Barron's* article. Short-selling indicators used to be widely followed and were very useful, but because of derivative trading and hedging strategies, they are no longer useful.

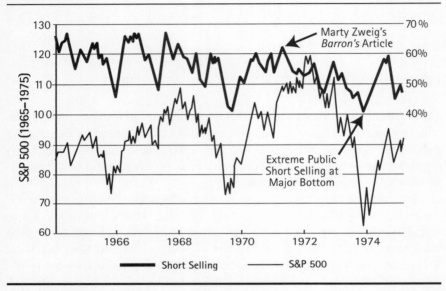

1966 to 1976. It measures the percentage of total short selling attributed to floor specialists. These short-selling indicators were extremely useful at signaling market tops and bottoms in the 1960s and 1970s, but they haven't worked since 1984, which marked the advent of program trading.

Program trading is the instantaneous buying and selling short of a stock or index to lock in an abnormal difference in price between two similar or identical investments. This type of short selling is done solely

---

Short selling is selling borrowed shares of stock under the expectation of being able to buy them back at a lower price and returning the shares you borrowed. This strategy makes money if prices decline and loses money if prices rise.

to lock in an investment gain; it does not indicate any expectation that prices are headed lower. Ultimately, this arbitrage short selling became so large that it introduced too much noise into the ratios, which made them useless. Although they are still followed, I do not recommend that anyone use the short-selling indicators any longer as a means to measure market sentiment.

The Put/Call Ratio

Another method of measuring investor activity is the put/call ratio. Officially, a *put* is an option to sell a stock at a specified price for a specified time. People buy puts if they expect the price of a stock to decline. A *call* is an option to buy a stock at a specified price for a specified time. People buy calls when they expect the price of a stock to advance. Because puts and calls can get very complicated, let's just say that puts are bets that stocks will decline, and calls are bets that they will advance. By calculating the ratio between the number of puts and calls, it is possible to get a good idea of what investors expect stock prices to do.

In 1970, before the creation of the Chicago Board Option Exchange (CBOE), the only available data on puts and calls was an informal option market put together by certain option dealers. It was Marty Zweig, in a couple of pioneering articles in *Barron's*, who analyzed the use of options as a measure of contrary opinion. The data necessary to follow these options, however, was difficult to come by. When formal option markets were established in the mid-1970s, it became much easier to track these ratios on a daily basis. I have been following them since the first year CBOE opened.

You can calculate two different ratios: the ratio of puts to calls for all individual stocks and the ratio of puts to calls for the index options. First, let's look at index options.

I remember dreaming in the late 1970s, about five years before their inception, that if index options were ever created it would be the perfect way to apply the theory of contrary opinion. When my dream was finally realized, I was disappointed; they never turned into the great indicator of contrary opinion I thought they would be. It was quite a disappointment.

On average, index put buying exceeds index call buying by as much as 2 : 1, but this ratio has been gradually rising over the years. For this reason, it's hard to establish the band that represents extremes in bullish or bearish sentiment. More importantly, the ratio has a tendency to go in the opposite direction from what you would expect. Studies seem to indicate that more institutions are using index options as market hedges, thereby skewing the numbers the way program trading skewed the short-selling ratios. Therefore, I do not use index options as an indicator.

NOTE

I know that the expansion in financial products over the last 20 years is good—I often trade the index options. However, from another point of view, I am disappointed to have lost first the old short-selling indicators and then the index options as good and reliable indicators for helping predict what the market is going to do. This is especially true as we enter a trading range market, when these tools would have been very useful.

The only indicator I use for studying the ratio of puts to calls is the ratio on individual stocks. This is the same basic method that Marty Zweig pioneered in 1970, and I believe it is still the best puts and calls indicator of investor sentiment. You can see this indicator in Figure 5.2. It usually goes high at market bottoms and low at market tops, following the pattern that you would expect from contrary opinion.

FIGURE 5.2   The Chicago Board Options Exchange puts-to-calls ratio from 1990 through 2000. A high ratio is 0.65; a low reading is 0.35.

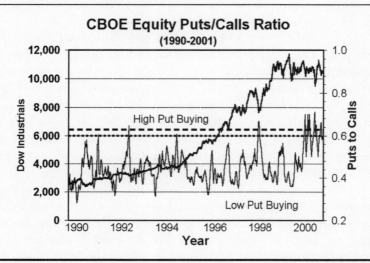

Newer Indicators

The VIX index and the Rydex mutual fund ratio of bull and bear fund money flows are two newer indicators of investor sentiment that have proved to have value. Unfortunately, they don't have a long track record to establish extreme readings through a number of bull and bear market cycles. What we have seen of them shows that they are very useful.

The Volatility Index (VIX).   The VIX index requires a bit of explanation. It is based on the theory of the price of options.

For many years no one knew how to price options. Then, about 30 years ago, three finance professors named Fisher Black, Myron Scholes, and Robert Merton came up with similar formulas. The formulas contained the strike price, an interest rate, the time remaining before expiration, and the volatility of the underlying stock. The last number, volatility, was one of the more important parameters in the equation. If a stock is extremely volatile, the price of the option must allow for that. In general, if one stock is twice as volatile as another, given everything else the same, an option on it should be twice as large.

How is this parameter (volatility) measured? Theoretically, it is measured by going back many months and calculating how much a stock moves around. The mathematical procedures for doing this are well established. For example, it is possible to calculate the volatility of the S&P 500 by going back over the last 12 months and calculating how much the S&P 500 moved above and below a certain average price. By doing this, we might calculate that it fluctuated by about 15% per year.

In theory, what investors are supposed to do is put this volatility number for the S&P 500 into the option equation along with the strike price and other factors and calculate the price they should pay for an option on the S&P 500. In practice, though, investors don't heed these theoretical calculations much. They have a tendency, especially when they get a strong opinion about the direction of the market, to buy options at almost any price. Because of this market technicians decided to turn the situation around and work the equations the other way. They take the current market price for the options and work backwards, calculating (using the option formulas) the implied volatility. In fact they do this with eight options to take out any anomaly, average the implied volatility of four close-to-expiration calls and four close-to-expiration puts.

This is the VIX: It is the implied volatility of the S&P index, but it isn't the S&P 500; it is the S&P 100, which is the original index used to trade index options. Originally, the S&P Corporation didn't want to risk the good name of the S&P 500 index by using it as a base for option trading. So they invested another index that would act just like it and used it instead; this was the S&P 100. Later, as option trading became more accepted and computer power increased, that all changed. Now almost every major index has options available, including the S&P 500. The VIX still measures, however, the implied volatility of the original S&P 100.

Figure 5.3 shows the VIX index plotted against the OEX. It is easy to see that local stock market bottoms occurs when speculators are pricing up the options and increasing the implied volatility. When prices have reached a peak, the implied volatility is low. The VIX has been calculated only back to 1993, so we don't have a long history of this index to determine what is high and what is low. So far, 20 is considered low and more than 35 is considered high. I do believe that, as long-term investor activity changes with the market, these extremes will change significantly. Only time will tell.

FIGURE 5.3 This graph plots the OEX index (the S&P 100) versus the implied volatility (the VIX) of the closest OEX options to expiration. We don't yet have enough history to identify extreme readings. What we do know so far is that when the VIX goes under 20, markets have made recent tops. Similarly, when the VIX has gone to a high of 35, that has signaled a local bottom. My experience tells me, however, that these high and low readings will change in the future as long-term investor activity increases or decreases and as the real underlying volatility of the S&P 100 also changes.

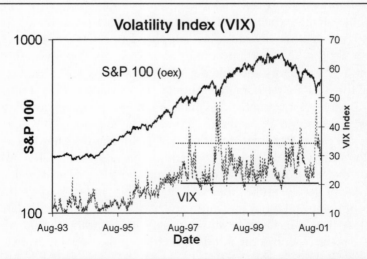

The Rydex Ratios.   The Rydex mutual fund family has several funds tied to the S&P 500 index including the Rydex Nova fund, which is leveraged to provide 150% exposure to the index, and the Rydex Ursa Fund, which goes up when the market goes down and provides the inverse performance of the index. This gives investors in the Rydex Family a big advantage—to invest and make money through either a bull market or bear market—as long as they can anticipate which fund to be in. Their shareholders are allowed to do unlimited exchanges between these funds. Carl Swenlin of Decisionpoint.com publishes a number of indicators based on Rydex fund information. One such indicator divides the dollars invested in the "bear" fund, Ursa, by dollars invested in Nova, the bullish fund. So far it acts like a very good contrary opinion indicator. When investors are pouring too much money in the bear fund and not much in the bull fund that is usually a sign of a bottom. Likewise, when they get too over invested in the bull fund that is a sign of a top.

Figure 5.4 shows the correlation between the S&P 500 and this bear/bull ratio. Since the data hasn't been available for more than a few years, there is not yet sufficient history to know what extreme readings in

---

FIGURE 5.4   The ratio of the amount of investor money that is in the Rydex Ursa Fund divided by the amount in the Rydex Nova Fund. Although there isn't enough history to formally establish what is a high or a low ratio, so far a ratio of 0.3 has occurred at a few major tops, while a ratio of 3.0 has occurred at a few major bottoms.

Rydex Data

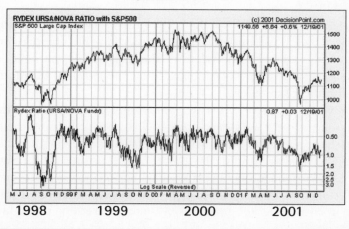

this index are. So far it seems that when the ratio is 0.3 that has indicated enough bullish sentiment to signal a top, while a ratio of 3.0 represents enough bearish sentiment to signal a major bottom. Again we'll have to see how this indicator develops to gain more confidence in it. But so far it seems to work pretty well. (The historical range has been 0.23 to 3.48.)

Second Method: Polling Services

The second method of measuring investor sentiment involves actually polling analysts and investors. Investor polling is being done by a number of services.

Futures Polling Services

Two or three services poll futures and commodity traders (people who buy and sell the stock market via index futures). The results of these polls show that futures traders are notoriously oriented to the short term. The numbers often go from a bullish extreme to a bearish extreme in just a few weeks. This fact highlights the importance of always knowing the time intention of the trade, as mentioned in Chapter 1. In my experience, futures polling information is useful only when you take long-term moving averages of the reading of each service and add them together. By combining the data in this way, you can produce a broader statistical foundation on which to base conclusions about investor sentiment. In general, unless I'm particularly interested in shorter-term movements, I avoid futures polling services because their data can be misleading.

The Guru Index

The oldest and most reliable of the polling services is called Investor's Intelligence, which was founded in 1963, to measure and compile the opinions of people who write newsletters about the stock market. Because the newsletter writers are often considered the gurus of the stock market, I call it the guru index.

Each week, Investor's Intelligence compiles and presents the percentage of newsletter writers who are bullish versus the percentage who are bearish (a third category of writers are those expecting just a correction, but I have never found this number to be useful). The bullish and bearish numbers have become a wonderful contrary opinion indicator because time has shown that newsletter writers often hold incorrect opinions at critical market junctures. Although it had one major failure in

FIGURE 5.5   This chart plots a 10-week moving average of the Investor's Intelligence percentage of newsletter writers who are bullish. The chart starts in 1963, with the earliest data available. You can see that extreme bullish sentiment exceeds 60%, and extreme bearish sentiment is shown by readings less than 30%. (Source: Investor's Intelligence, 30 Church St., New Rochelle, NY 10801; phone (914) 632-0422.)

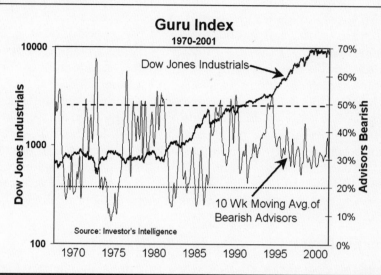

1974, when it failed to predict the last major wave down in the bear market of 1973 to 1974, the overall history of the guru index as a contrary opinion indicator is very good. In practice, I take 10-week moving averages of these percentages to help smooth out the readings. When I refer to the guru indicator, I'm referring to a 10-week average of either the bullish readings or the bearish ones. Sometimes it is better to highlight one side or the other when presenting the data to people. Figure 5.5 shows the 10-week moving average of the percentage of the bearish newsletter writers charted back to 1970.

Sometimes technicians use the Investor's Intelligence bearish reading more than the bullish ones, or they take ratios of the two. However, I have found this to be an unnecessary finesse. The simple bullish or bearish reading works quite well, and it is also easier for most people to understand. However, to test the theory of contrary opinion explained in the next section, I used the percentage of bearish newsletter writers.

THE THEORY OF CONTRARY OPINION: THE PROOF

As I explained in Chapter 1, the stock market I subscribe to holds that prices are random and unpredictable most of the time, except at certain moments, when they can become predictable. In my experience, the best way to discover these predictable moments is to use contrary opinion. I've learned this after many years in the stock market. However, it's one thing to say this and another to prove it. So, I performed an intriguing study using the Investor's Intelligence bearish readings. I believe this study proves the statement that the market is random most of the time but predictable when sentiment is at extremes.

The assumption in this study was this: If sentiment is useful at predicting the market, I would find that the market did well after extremely high bearish readings and poorly after extremely low bearish readings. Readings between extremes should show no correlation. On the other hand, if sentiment wasn't useful at all and the market was completely random, I would see no correlation of any kind. All I would see was average market performance, regardless of the sentiment reading.

Gathering Data

I began the data series in 1970, when Investor's Intelligence started weekly sentiment readings. I calculated the 10-week moving average of the percentage of advisors who were bearish for every week from 1970 to 1998. I then calculated how the stock market performed over the 6 months following each reading. For example, I'd calculate the 10-week moving average for January 1, and then calculate how the market did from January 1 to June 31. Then, I'd calculate the 10-week average for the next week, January 7, and determine how the market did over the next six months, from January 7 to July 7. Altogether, I surveyed a total of 1,447 weeks in the 29 years of data, yielding 1,447 sentiment readings and 1,447 corresponding 6-month performance numbers.

I then divided the results into groups, with each group representing a tight bracketing of the sentiment reading. I did this in order to see how the market performs after extreme readings, so I located all the times the guru index showed a certain low range of readings and then calculated the stock market's performance for those readings. For example, the first grouping comprised all the times bearish sentiment was between zero and 10% (historically, an extremely low level of bearish sentiment). Over 28 years, such a low level of bearish sentiment occurred only 13 times.

The average stock market return for these 13 times was –5%. Bearish readings of 10% to 20% (again extremely low) occurred 200 times, and the average performance for these 200 times was zero. Readings between 20% and 30% occurred 309 times, and the average 6-month performance was 7.7%. Readings between 30% and 40% occurred 482 times, and the average return was 13.9%. Readings between 40% and 50% occurred 310 times, and the result was 6.9%. Readings between 50% and 60% (levels of extremely high bearish sentiment) occurred 118 times, and the average 6-month result was 22.8%. There were only 15 times when the reading went higher than 60%, and the average return 6 months later was 25.3%. The average return from the Dow Jones industrials over the 28 years was 8.8%. (Note: These results do not take dividends into account, but their inclusion would not change the results of the study. They would lift all the total return numbers a little but would not change the relative performance of each group with respect to the average Dow Jones return.)

The study went into much greater detail than this, but the data I've given here is enough to make my point. The chart in Figure 5.6 summarizes the results just presented. The chart plots the grouping of bearish sentiment (on the X-axis) against the average 6-month market gain for that grouping. The 6-month returns have been annualized.

Examining the Results

As Figure 5.6 shows, the performance of the stock market correlates well with extremes in sentiment. Market performance after extremely low bearish sentiment (newsletter writers expecting higher prices) was much lower than average. Market performance after extremely high bearish sentiment (newsletter writers expecting low prices) was much higher than average. Sentiment readings between these extremes showed little correlation with market performance.

As you'll recall, I explained in Chapter 4 the dangers of using technical indicators to predict markets beyond 6 to 9 months. Because sentiment is classified as a technical indicator, if this caution explains why I measured the market performance over six months rather than a year. Because it is a technical type of indicator, contrary opinion is to have predictive value, it should probably correlate best with movements lasting from 6 to 9 months.

Even so, with contrary opinion it is sometimes acceptable to make an exception to the 6-month rule and use the sentiment readings to forecast

FIGURE 5.6   The plotted points represent the average Dow Jones return for six months (on average) for seven different sentiment groupings. This 28-year study shows that the stock prices outperform when newsletter writers are extremely bearish (right two points) and under perform when there is an extreme lack of bearishness (left two points). Sentiment readings that are not extreme (middle three points) show little correlation with market moves as one would expect.

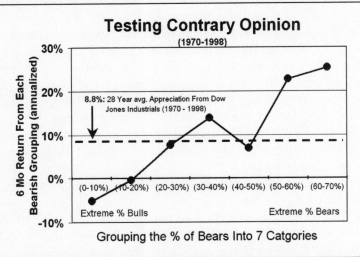

longer-term trends, which would occur when the indicators go to very extreme readings. At those times, I think it's fair to stretch the point somewhat and presuppose that sentiment can be used to signal a major bull or bear market. This is especially true *if the extremes in sentiment are also occurring during a period of extreme public interest and speculation in the stock market.*

THE THEORY IN PRACTICE

Something as powerful as contrary opinion has many applications, and using contrary opinion to help determine market trends is also a fine art. The following sections explain what I've learned about it over the years, especially its capability for determining where you are in the Elliott wave cycle.

Keep in mind that the theory of contrary opinion holds only when there are extremes in sentiment. In practice, many market technicians make the mistake of attempting to apply the theory before sentiment (whether bearish or bullish) has reached an extreme. I know because I've made that mistake enough to know that it can be a major weakness. In general, I found myself doing this when the market was in a highly unpredictable state and I was pressing to know what it was saying.

For example, suppose the market enters a sideways trading range and it is not yet clear exactly which way the market will go. The trading range lasts for a long time and you get impatient. You look at the sentiment readings and find that 55% are bullish and 45% are bearish, at which point you might conclude, since more people are bullish than bearish, that prices are ready to break out of their trading range and decline. This would be a mistake. You should hold your ground and just accept the fact that investor sentiment, at that moment, does not indicate anything. Wait until the picture becomes clearer; it almost always will.

Using the Theory

When I first began studying the market I thought that contrary opinion was useful only for finding major market tops and bottoms in movements that last from six months to a year. I thought the best approach was to wait for an extreme reading to signal the start of a movement (whether up or down) and then wait for an opposite extreme reading to signal the end of the movement. I assumed that a major market movement wouldn't begin or end until an extreme reading had occurred. Although I still generally believe this, I've found some other ways of using contrary opinion that are just as helpful. It would be hard to test these methods (as I did the Investor's Intelligence data), but personal experience has proved them useful.

For example, I have found that contrary opinion is very useful at determining whether, after a really good advance, the market will go still higher. For instance, suppose the market has had a good upward run for two or three months and then goes into a sudden three-day sell-off. Now, for any advance that has sustaining power, there will always be a wall of doubt and worry, except near the very end. So in this situation, you need to watch the put/call ratio and at the same time, keep track of what the market commentators on television and radio are saying. If the market is to push forward, you will hear a chorus of analysts claiming that the market is now finally ready for its correction. Such a sudden increase in caution is good. From my experience with contrary opinion, it is clear that the market will probably continue higher.

Let us look at this in a little more detail. Quite often, after a long run-up, there is a sudden sharp sell-off that quickly stops and then begins a slow recovery to its previous highs, at which point it stalls and begins a second sell-off. This second sell-off (the final C leg of an ABC correction, as you will learn in Chapter 6) usually generates much more skepticism because more people think that the last rally was the rally that failed and the run-up is over. The market acts like prices are rounding over, and beginning a larger decline. At such a time, be sure to watch the put/call ratio very closely. If the ratio suddenly increases with more put buying, the movement is probably a sideways correction before another lengthy thrust (Figure 5.7). However, if put buying doesn't increase and there continues to be high call buying, be very careful, because there is probably more movement behind the correction. *Always pay close attention*

FIGURE 5.7 Watch for a rapid rise in bearish sentiment during a sideways correction after an extended advance. It is a good signal that the rally will continue.

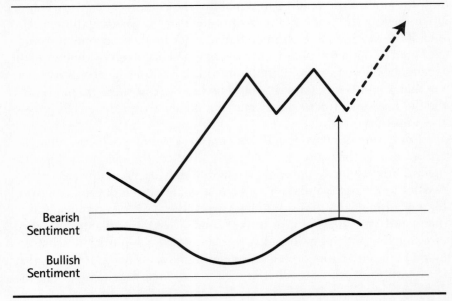

anytime you observe a widely held belief that a market correction has begun and yet prices are only a few days away from possibly breaking to new highs—that is a strong market.

How the Theory Helped in Navigating the 1994 to 1999 Market

Let's look at one use of contrary opinion that helped my clients stay almost fully invested through the great bull market of 1994 to 1999. The story starts in December of 1994, when at my year-end client seminars, I pulled out the Investor's Intelligence readings for the first time. I did this because the Investor's Intelligence reading was showing the highest bearish sentiment since the bottom in 1987—equal in bearish sentiment to major bear market bottoms. I told my clients this probably meant a major advance was imminent, so they should stay put with their stock investments. I explained contrary opinion to them, much as I have throughout this chapter. After the move started, we religiously provided updates of the Investor's Intelligence readings at our client seminars every six months.

One fact kept hitting us in the face: As the advance continued, we noted no swing toward the type of extreme bullish sentiment readings that would indicate a market top. In fact, the bullish readings stayed very muted, and they were accompanied by magazine articles illustrated with pictures of bears, in which many analysts argued that the market was overvalued. These naysayers represented the well-known wall of worry (Figure 5.8). True to what I said in the beginning of this chapter, we kept the theory of contrary opinion senior to any data about the economy. It was highly unusual, and to us much more important, to have such a visible wall of worry than to worry about the market being overvalued. So, we just stayed with this bullish idea, and in this case, it worked very well.

Understanding the Consensus Opinion and How It Changes

It is important to watch how quickly investors change their opinions about market direction. As a general rule, a rapid and sudden change in investor sentiment when the market starts into a correction or rally means that the prior trend will soon continue. This is particularly true in bear market rallies.

For instance, suppose the market has had a severe three-month decline. High bearish sentiment registers at the bottom. The market hits a

FIGURE 5.8   The wall of worry. It is an old cliché that markets continue to rise against a wall of worry and doubt. You could actually see this cliché in action from 1994 to 1999 by watching the guru index, Investor's Intelligence. Bullish sentiment refused to rise above 50% until the beginning of 1999, when the wall finally broke.

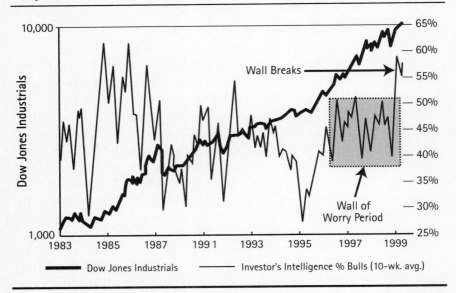

level, stays there for a few weeks, and then starts a sudden rally. If during this rally sentiment goes rapidly to the bullish side and stays there, you can assume that it is only a bear market rally (rather than a sustained upward move) and that another leg down is imminent. As a rule, sustainable rallies off market bottoms hold the bearish sentiment even as the market rallies. There should always be a wall of worry and disbelief as the market works higher.

It is important to pay attention to analysts' opinions in the press. Market analysts on television or radio are talking to a mass audience and so will generally make only statements with which their audience will agree. Both their caution and their enthusiasm generally reflect the overall feelings of the investing public. Therefore, *don't pay any attention to the reasons these commentators present!* Tabulate *only* the overall conclusions (bullish or bearish) of the viewpoints being broadcast. Although these conclusions can be difficult to quantify, they are sometimes extremely useful as a confirming indication of a statistical measure.

Finding Correlations between Group Emotions and Market Volume

It is important to understand emotions because they govern and regulate almost all human activity, which includes the human activity of investing. They are also thought to be one of the causes behind the instabilities of feedback loops. People like to say that two emotions drive the market: fear and greed. However, this simplistic picture is incomplete and doesn't explain what is actually observed. For one thing, greed isn't an emotion, it's a vice. Furthermore, a great many other emotions are manifested in the stock market besides fear.

For example, investors can become emotionally apathetic about investing, especially after a major bear market. What kind of volume would you expect if most investors were in the state of apathy? Very low volume. I've seen angry markets, a phenomenon that usually occurs when investors become frustrated after missing a large price movement and have been waiting for a correction that hasn't come. They get angry and charge the market, buying in a huge surge of volume and paying any price.

Because of the strong correlation between an emotion and the character of the activity associated with it, you can often measure the group emotions of investors by closely following volume. Table 5.1 summarizes a few emotions and the volume characteristics expected from groups in each emotional state. Such factors are important because major tops and bottoms of the market are usually associated with investors manifesting certain group emotions. Certain volume patterns evolve that can be explained by the action of group emotions.

Bear markets, for example, often end in selling climaxes. Volume builds when fear and panic set in as prices plunge but this emotion is soon followed by the emotion of apathy (complete demoralization),

TABLE 5.1   Group emotion and market volume

Emotion	Volume Characteristics
Excitement, enthusiasm	Constant high volume
Fear	High, rising volume
Boredom*	Relatively low, flat volume
Anger, frustration	Suddenly rising volume
Apathy, low interest	Very low, flat volume

*Normally found during long, fourth wave corrections (see Chapter 7)

which produces very low volume. It is best to buy into this low volume. It's also common for investors to lapse into a state of boredom as the market moves into a long consolidation after a lengthy advance. In such a situation, volume will dwindle during the boredom phase. The market can stay in this state for some time.

Of particular interest is the emotion of enthusiasm or exhilaration, which shows up during the final stages of a protracted bull market and accompanies high levels of speculation. The effects of enthusiasm usually play out something like this: After a long period of advancing stock prices, investors get the feeling that making money is easy, and so they start to feel cocky. After seeing many examples of small stocks or highly speculative investments rising dramatically in value, investors lose their normal caution and become willing to gamble on these seemingly sure things. As a result, the volume activity in these investments rises dramatically compared to more stable, investment-quality issues.

Market students and analysts still have much more to learn about the complicated relationships between group emotions and stock investing.

RESISTANCE TO APPLYING THE THEORY

I've made a clear case for the value of the theory of contrary opinion in predicting intermediate-term movements of the stock market. If the stock market is predictable, as my model holds, the ability to predict it lies in understanding and applying contrary opinion. Of all technical indicators, sentiment is by far the most valuable tool. Nevertheless, as we have seen, it presents problems.

Through my seminars, I have found that the general public sees the logic of the theory of contrary opinion but nonetheless, refuses to take it seriously; therefore, investors have trouble applying it. Why? Because to apply the theory, you have to ignore the pressing economic circumstances that are making the vast majority of investors either bullish or bearish. You have to be willing to say, "The economic scenario that everyone is talking about must be wrong, even though it seems so obviously right." Since most people consider economic data more important than the fact that there is an extreme reading in sentiment, investors find it hard to ignore the obvious economic picture and go with contrary opinion.

I often hear clients say, "Yes, we know everyone is currently bullish, but this time there's a good reason to feel that way." *That is always the problem!* As I said in the beginning of this chapter, *you will successfully apply the theory of contrary opinion only if you elevate it to a senior position above any economic data.*

How can BABES and O'BUCS really be the way things are? I don't fully understand it myself, but I can describe it and tell you that history shows that it is this way, but I can't tell you exactly why. What I have learned, however, is that the stock market tells a story by its price action. The long-term price pattern has an economic reason behind it, a financial story that evolves over time and makes sense in terms of stock prices.

The situation resembles a novel in which the author has hidden clues to the ending extremely well. Only near the end of the book does the whole story suddenly become clear. The stock market story is written in a special book, however, in that when everyone sees the story, it ceases to exist as the story; the final pages just disappear. At that moment of recognition, few notice that a new book has been pulled out and a new story has begun. Investment success goes to individuals who can see the correct story before the next person.

The only explanation I have is this. At any point, there are two forces at work in the market: One builds the economy up; the other tears it down. These two forces coexist and the price of stocks always reflects the consensus viewpoint on which of the two is dominant. In truth, however, people have a tendency toward sloppy thinking. At critical market junctures, if you key off investor sentiment and study the situation deeply enough, usually you can find holes in the consensus thinking. Some great traders, the geniuses, spot these holes naturally and quickly. George Soros and Warren Buffet come to mind. They seem to see the correct but opposing view, the O'BUCS idea, almost instinctively.

In applying contrary opinion, when you observe extreme sentiment, you must reject the consensus story and search for the new, correct, emerging story—and have confidence that it will be there. This is the key.

6

Price Patterns, Fractals, and Mr. Elliott

The first five chapters explained the model I use to understand stock market movements and integrated technical and fundamental analysis into the framework of that model. According to that model, stock prices equal a fair value that is modified and stretched by that action of three feedback loops in three different time domains. Each time domain can become unstable by itself, which can trigger a feedback-loop price movement in that domain. Sometimes these movements can affect each other since there is a degree of interdependency.

It is my belief that this model opens the door to a predictable stock market. Chapter 5 explained that these predictable moments for the stock market are best located using the theory of contrary opinion.

Theoretically, the interplay of the four elements of the model—a fair value term evolving over time as the economy changes and the three feedback loops—are the forces that produce the minute-to-minute, day-to-day, week-to-week, and year-to-year price movements. The zigzag price movement from minutes to years is simply the result of the interplay of these four components. In this chapter, you will learn about several additional ideas that open up a greater understanding of these patterns.

The last 20 years ushered in a new era of discovery in mathematics, physics, and finance. One of these discoveries has application to understanding stock price patterns: the concept of fractals. The link between the theory of fractals and stock prices is forged from two fascinating facts.

After the discovery of fractals in the 1970s, people started noticing that stock prices produced charts with patterns that fit the definition of a fractal. Mathematicians had discovered that fractal patterns occur in systems that are composed of feedback loops. People knew that the stock market behaved at times like a feedback loop, so its fractal nature wasn't a surprise.

More startling is that fact that a fractal theory for stock prices (the Elliott wave theory) was actually developed in the 1930s—40 years before the theory of fractals was formulated by Benoit Mandelbrot! This chapter explains what fractals are as well as the Elliott wave theory—the first fractal theory for stocks—finally establishing a theoretical foundation for this controversial theory.

ORIGINAL PRICE PATTERN OBSERVATIONS

The accepted models of the stock market, such as the efficient market model, give no good explanation for the patterns we see in stock charts. The usual interpretation is that these jerks and starts are the sudden adjustments to fair value as news about companies continuously streams in. The new model presented earlier in this book gives a different interpretation. It says that economic news does cause price adjustments, but it also triggers instabilities, setting into motion the interplay of the three feedback loops. The vibratory price pattern we see is the concurrent sum of all these effects.

People have learned that they should always pay close attention to anything that is observed over many generations. Buried in those observations is usually something very important, and when that truth finally surfaces, it can be quite illuminating. The Elliott wave idea appears to have come into being in just this way; it seems to be the culmination of observations made by many people over many years. The seminal observations of Charles Dow and W.D. Gann underlie what eventually became the Elliott wave theory.

Reviewing the Dow Theory of Price Movement

The story begins with Charles Dow, whose observations and thoughts at the turn of the century later became known as the Dow theory of price movement. Although the theory is generally considered old-fashioned now, careful study shows that it is surprisingly modern and contains most of the basics of today's technical analysis. Discussing the entire Dow theory is beyond the scope of this book, but I do cover the part concerning price patterns. The following paragraph is from Robert Rhea's book *The Dow Theory*, written in 1932.

> The Primary Bull Market: A primary bull market is a broad upward movement, interrupted by secondary reactions, and averaging longer than two years. During this time, stock prices advance because of a demand created by both investment and speculative buying caused by improving business conditions and increased speculative activity. *There are three phases of a bull period: the first is represented by reviving confidence in the future of business, the second is the response of stock prices to the known improvement in corporation earnings, and the third is the period when speculation is rampant and inflation apparent—a period when stocks are advanced on hopes and expectations.* [Italics added.]

Reviewing W.D. Gann's Observations

Another well-known advisor and market technician, W.D. Gann, had a trading career that began near the turn of the century and lasted more than 45 years. His observations about stock market price patterns were very similar to those of Charles Dow.

> Stock market campaigns move in three to four sections or waves. Never consider that the market has reached final top when it makes the first section in a move up, because if it is a real Bull Market it will run at least three sections and possibly four before a final high is reached.

> We explore Gann's comment about the possible fourth wave later in this chapter.

Combining the Dow and Gann Patterns

Now that we have that simple background, let's draw Charles Dow's and W.D. Gann's observations. In Figure 6.1, you can see the bull market structure that both Dow and Gann describe: a pattern composed of three sections interrupted by two secondary corrections. Neither Dow nor Gann saw any repeating pattern or definable structure other than these

FIGURE 6.1 The three movements of a bull market, as described by Charles Dow and W.D. Gann.

three simple movements; they considered short-term movements random and unimportant.

The major drawback to Dow's and Gann's observations is that there is no financial theory to explain them. They are simply empirical observations, without any supporting structure, begging for an explanation. That's not to say the observations are not useful; it means only that we don't know why this pattern occurs. However, even without a theoretical foundation, any real effort to predict the stock market must somehow address this long-observed phenomenon.

It would seem that any observation made repeatedly over such a long period has to contain some fundamental truth since it is constant against the ever-changing economic picture. As a physicist would say, "It is an observation that seems to measure something that is time invariant" and physicists always look for things that stay the same when everything else changes. When they find something that stays constant when everything else changes, it is always an important discovery.

However, without a supporting theory that would explain why a bull market contains three sections, why limit the existence of price patterns to the bull-market level? If we look a little harder, we might discover other repeating price patterns over other time frames and, from this higher level of observation, develop an explanation or theory for the patterns. Enter a man named R.N. Elliott (Figure 6.2).

FIGURE 6.2   R.N. Elliott developed the first fractal theory of stock prices in 1937, 40 years before the discovery of fractals. (Source: Reproduced by permission from *R.N. Elliott's Masterworks*, edited by Robert R. Prechter, Jr. © 1994, Robert R. Prechter, Jr.)

R.N. ELLIOTT

R.N. Elliott, an accountant, formulated his observations of the wave principle during a long period of convalescence during the 1930s. He started with the basic ideas of Gann and Dow, but he went much further. Mathematicians today would recognize the theory that he formulated in the 1930s as a fractal theory.

I first learned about the Elliott wave theory in 1979, from Robert Prechter's book *Elliott Wave Principle—Key to Market Behavior*. Now, after applying the Elliott wave theory for more than 20 years, I believe I'm in a position to explain the power and the limitations of this interesting theory. It has received some negative press from market analysts who tried to make it into more than it really is and who pushed the theory beyond what it is capable of doing. This caused numerous forecasting failures, which tended to invalidate the theory in the eyes of many people.

Expanding on the Dow-Gann Bull-Market Pattern

To describe Elliott's deeper observations, let's start with the basic three-section Dow-Gann pattern for a bull market diagrammed in Figure 6.1. As you look at the pattern, consider the first of the three sections. Neither Dow nor Gann saw any deeper underlying pattern in this simple upward movement; it was simply the first extended, advancing period of the bull market. In contrast, Elliott said that if you looked a little closer, you would see a similar pattern there, too. The first movement of the bull market is actually composed of three smaller movements of its own. In the second section of the bull market are three additional smaller movements. The same is also true of the third section. Figure 6.3 illustrates the finer detail that Elliott observed in the three advancing waves of a bull market.

Elliott expanded his observations. Where Dow and Gann saw no pattern to the two corrections separating the three waves, Elliott did. According to him, these corrections didn't just go down, they were composed of two declining waves separated by a little rally. In other words, a correction is seldom one sell-off but two. Figure 6.3 diagrams both these observations in the complete Elliott wave pattern for a bull market, showing the down-up-down pattern of the two corrections that separate the three advancing waves.

FIGURE 6.3 The expanded pattern for a bull market, as seen by R.N. Elliott, including the pattern for the corrections that separate the primary waves. Also shown is the wave structure of the bear market that follows the three advancing waves of the bull market.

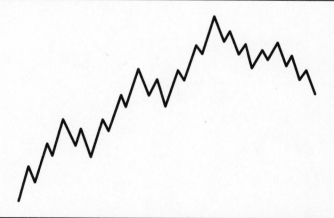

Elliott even found a price pattern for bear markets—something no one else had ever done. He considered a bear market a correction of the bull market and, like all corrections, it should have two down waves, separated by a rally (the bear market rally). Furthermore, these two down waves break up, like all other price movements, into smaller movements, as Figure 6.3 shows.

At this point Elliott (although he didn't know it) made the leap into fractals. He said that the three waves that make up each of the three sections of the primary bull market also have a structure. You guessed it— each of the three waves is composed of three smaller movements. The corrective movements that separate these three also have the same pattern as the earlier correction: two down waves separated by a small rally.

Figure 6.4 shows the breakdown of these patterns into their next level of smaller movements. In this figure, you can see the basic Elliott wave pattern, showing three levels of the basic pattern; this is the very essence of the Elliott wave principle. When can a movement not be broken down into three smaller movements? According to Elliott, never. Any stock price movement can be broken into three sections of smaller price changes and time lengths. This is true of movements over days, hours, or even minutes.

FIGURE 6.4   On closer examination, it becomes apparent that each section, or wave, in the price pattern also consists of three smaller waves. Similarly, the movements of each correction can be subdivided into finer movements.

Patterns Bigger than Bull Markets

Elliott expanded on this idea of continuously repeating patterns, but this time he went in the other direction. He said that the three-wave repeating doesn't stop at a bull market. According to his theory, what we usually call a bull market is just one section of a larger three-section movement. Similarly, three of these much larger movements come together to form an even larger three-wave movement. He called these larger-than-a-bull-market movements *cycles*, *super* cycles, and *grand super cycles*.

The accepted belief among Elliott wave practitioners is that the longest known cycle, called the grand super cycle, started in 1790, when the New York Stock Exchange was formed. Each advancing wave in this grand super cycle is about 50 years or longer and is composed of many bull markets (Figure 6.5).

FIGURE 6.5   The longest known cycle—Elliott's the grand super cycle—started in 1790. Many Elliott wave practitioners believe that the grand super cycle is nearing an end. (Source: Reproduced by permission from *Elliott Wave Principle— Key to Market Behavior,* by Robert R. Prechter Jr. and Alfred John Frost. © 1978–2000 Robert R. Prechter Jr.)

Reproduced by permission from *Elliot Wave Principle—Key to Market Behavior,* by Robert R. Prechter, Jr. and Alfred John Frost. Copyright 1978–2000 Robert R. Prechter, Jr.

THE ELLIOTT WAVE THEORY VERSUS THE REAL MARKET

Let's see how Elliott applied the theory to the real stock market. We'll use an example from Elliott's original works (Figure 6.6). The great stock market crash of 1929 hit bottom in the summer of 1932, at which point the market began a 5-year bull market. Notice how Elliott labeled the waves. You can see that the waves are nowhere near the same size in terms of price or time duration as those in the idealized wave pattern. For example, the first advance lasted 3 months, the second advance lasted 5 months, and the third lasted 31 months. Therefore, we can understand that the simple patterns building up into larger patterns might be much more difficult to determine in practice. Unfortunately, this is true. Interpreting the waves in the real world is always very difficult and requires adding a few ideas that help bridge the gap from the ideal pattern to the real pattern that stock prices make. These nuances include things called extensions, irregular corrections, horizontal corrections, and fifth-wave diagonal triangles.

FIGURE 6.6 The 1932 to 1938 stock market, as labeled by R.N. Elliott. The chart plots the monthly range of the Dow Jones industrials. His labeling of the long extension wave from 1934 to 1937 as ABCDE does not follow the current protocol of using numbers for the advancing waves.

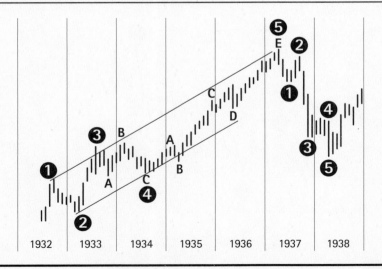

Labeling Elliott's Waves

Notice that describing Elliott's concept of sections within sections within sections can become a little confusing—it's easy to get lost in the various waves. Up to this point, I've intentionally avoided the normal Elliott wave labeling to accentuate the similarities between his observations and those of Dow and Gann. The basic advancing movement in the Elliott pattern consists of three advancing sections separated by two corrections. The waves are labeled 1, 2, 3, 4, and 5. Waves 1, 3, and 5 are advancing, and waves 2 and 4 are corrective.

A correction follows at the end of wave 5. The correction has three waves or sections labeled A, B, and C. A and C are the downward moves, and B is the separating rally. Movements of different degrees are distinguished by numbers, numbers within circles, numbers within brackets, and so on. In the ABC parts of the correction, capital letters, small letters, letters within circles, letters within brackets, and so on are used, although there is no established procedure for the labeling. In Figure 6.7, I have labeled the three degrees seen in the basic Elliott wave pattern.

FIGURE 6.7 The varying levels of the Elliott wave pattern are differentiated using variations on the basic 12345ABC labels. Shown are three levels of the basic pattern, with corresponding numbers and letters.

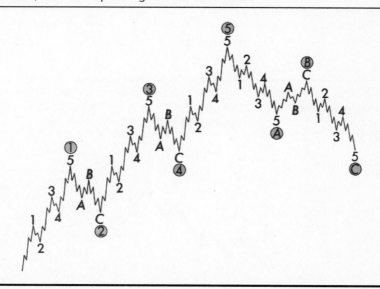

NOTE
The waves, or cycles, of the Elliott wave pattern are not time cycles, like sound or sine waves; they are action cycles. Eight events must occur before a cycle is complete. These eight events—12345ABC—do not have to be of the same size or duration.

The Elliott Wave Variations

Before we can apply the Elliott wave theory to the real stock market, we need to know more about the variations of the ideal pattern. These allow us to fit the theoretical pattern closer to the real patterns the market makes.

Extensions

We know that if the market does follow the Elliott wave pattern, it would have to be a stretched and compressed version of the idealized pattern. One way the Elliott wave can be stretched is for one of the three forward waves (waves 1, 3, or 5) to become much larger than the other two. You saw an extension in Figure 6.6, where wave 5 was the extended wave. Because an extension wave is larger and longer than the other two, the five waves that form the extension are also much larger. In fact, they can get so large that they can be as big in price and time movement as the other two primary waves (Figure 6.8).

When an extension exists in one of the waves, the whole movement seems to be made up of five thrusting waves, not three. Extensions usu-

---

FIGURE 6.8 An Elliott wave variation called an extension, in which one of the primary waves (wave 3 here) can be so large that the smaller movements that make it up become almost as large as the other two primary waves.

FIGURE 6.9   In an Elliott wave variation called a flat, waves A and C end up at the same level.

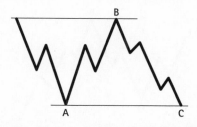

ally occur in waves 3 or 5—especially wave 3, but they seldom occur in wave 1. They never occur in two similar waves of a movement. Extensions occur during powerful market periods, such as the big advance from 1994 to 1998. Unfortunately, there is no known way to anticipate an extension.

The Flat

The corrective waves 2 and 4 show the greatest amount of variation and, I have found, cause the most amount of trouble. The simple ABC structure, as drawn by Elliott in the idealized pattern, is seldom seen. What is seen is a slight variation on this pattern, called a *flat*. In the basic Elliott diagram that is usually drawn, wave C goes lower than wave A. A flat occurs when waves A and C end up at the same level (Figure 6.9). You can see that the basic ABC idea is still there, but the size and endpoint are different, as are the internal movements that comprise each section.

The Irregular Correction

One of the most interesting variations on a flat occurs when the B wave continues up and actually exceeds the top of wave 5 (Figure 6.10). This variation is called an *irregular correction*, and because the market makes a new high on wave B, it gives the impression that the overall movement is composed of four sections rather than three. It also explains what W.D. Gann meant by "three sections and possibly four": he was observing what we now know is an irregular correction.

The difference between an irregular correction taking the market to new highs versus a normal thrusting wave is that the B wave is made up of three movements rather than the usual five. This is very important and helps distinguish the B wave from a normal thrusting movement.

FIGURE 6.10   An Elliott wave variation called an irregular correction, in which the B wave continues up and exceeds the top of the preceding wave 5.

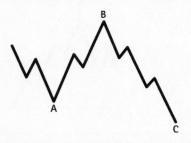

Horizontal Triangle

Quite often, the fourth-wave correction can have a much more complex pattern than normal, forming what is called a *horizontal triangle* or wedge (Figure 6.11). A horizontal triangle almost always happens when the corrective wave 2 is small and wave 3 turns into an extension. When this happens, we have the picture of a huge, long advance with a small wave 2 correction; a large and long correction is now overdue. It's as if the whole correction for the move takes place in wave 4, therefore wave

FIGURE 6.11   A horizontal triangle usually occurs as a fourth-wave correction after a long runup. It's as if all the correction for the whole move is being saved for one long fourth wave. A horizontal correction is composed of five movements (1, 2, 3, 4, and 5) and is not a normal ABC correction.

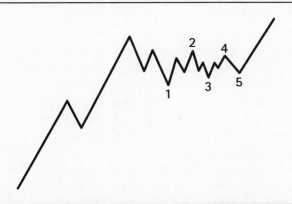

4 stretches out into a long sideways movement. It still has the 13 sub-waves of the standard correction, but they are altered a little into a longer sideways pattern. This type of correction is important because I believe the market has entered into one at this writing.

SEARCHING FOR AN UNDERLYING THEORY

If the real market exactly followed the perfectly drawn wave pattern, the market would be completely predictable; we would know exactly what was coming next—and when. The real market doesn't behave that way, and the Elliott wave theory acknowledges this. Elliott wave theorists believe that the basic pattern is always there; they think that if you add a few more ideas to the theory and study it hard enough, you can discover that pattern.

Elliott wave theorists say that the real stock market *is* the idealized curve, just stretched and pulled out of shape a little. If Elliott wave practitioners are right, it means that the basic pattern is there and that the market is generally predictable; if they are wrong and deluding themselves, the patterns are just a random jumble of zigzags and the market is unpredictable.

Elliott searched for an underlying theory that explained his wave principle. Because fractals were not known at the time, his ideas centered on the medieval mathematics of Fibonacci, whose number series matches the ever-expanding counts of the wave pattern. The only applicable idea that came from Fibonacci is a ratio called the *golden mean*, which is 1.618. Over the years Elliott wave theorists have tried to make the ratios of the size of price movements or the ratios of the time span behind these movements equal to the golden mean. I have never found that it worked.

Elliott had the right idea in looking for an underlying theory that would explain his observation of waves within waves within waves, a theory that would support his octave pattern (12345ABC) repeating from the very small time scales up to the very large. He was too far ahead of his time, though; the underlying theory had not been developed yet.

I was giving a seminar in 1982 about the Elliott wave theory when someone came up afterward and told me I had been describing fractals. I looked into it, learned what fractals are, and found out that the Elliott wave theory is exactly that—a fractal theory. Fractals are the correct underlying foundation for the whole wave principle.

A Guiding Principle

The failure of trying to make the ratios of either the size or the duration of price movements equal to the golden mean (1.618) confirmed an earlier conclusion of mine. Any simple ratio is just that—it's too simple—and therefore it couldn't possibly work. My reasoning is very practical: If such a simple ratio worked, it would have been discovered years ago by one of the hundreds of thousands of intelligent people who have pored over investment numbers for the last two centuries. I think the fact that no one has ever discovered a simple ratio shows that probably none exists.

Based on this reasoning, I established a guiding principle for myself. A correct theory of the stock market must be complicated enough to make the market unpredictable most of the time (so that simple ratios don't work) and predictable only part of the time. Therefore, a correct theory cannot be too simple; it has to be somewhat complex. We hope, however, that it's not too complicated to discover.

FRACTALS: THE THEORY BEHIND THE ELLIOTT WAVE PATTERNS

What is a fractal? Benoit Mandelbrot, the mathematician who discovered fractals, defines a *fractal* as "a geometrical shape that can be separated into parts, where the shape of every part is a reduced-scale version of the whole" ("A Fractal Walk Down Wall Street," *Scientific American*, February 1999). Essentially, if you take any little part of the whole and magnify it until it is the same size as the whole, that little part now looks like and has all the characteristics of the whole.

Stock price charts are this way. If you were to take a weekly chart of the stock market for 50 years, isolate any week and magnify up the price fluctuations showing the minute-by-minute price changes, you would find the same jiggles and patterns in the one-week period as in the 50-year period. If you took away the time scale at the bottom and the prices on the side and laid the two periods side by side, you wouldn't be able to

A *fractal*, according to Benoit Mandelbrot, is "a geometrical shape that can be separated into parts, where the shape of every part is a reduced-scale version of the whole."

tell which was the minute-by-minute chart and which was the 50-year chart (there is a subtle way to tell between extreme time scales, but that has no value to us here).

The subject of fractals is an important new advancement in our understanding of the geometrical patterns formed in nature. Their study is considered a branch of chaos theory and has wide application in many fields. Besides helping explain stock price movements, fractals also shed light on the distribution of galaxies in the universe, the structure of blood vessels in the body, the patterns of coastlines, and many previously confusing mathematical curves.

Stock Price Patterns Are Like Fractals

Stock prices follow the fractal definition. Let's take a time view of the S&P 500—for example, 50 days. Then let's take a little section out of this, such as what the market did minute by minute during one day. If you magnify the minute-by-minute chart to the same size as the 50-day chart, they look the same (Figure 6.12). With stock prices, you can't tell whether you are looking at a 10-year sweep, with the back-and-forth fluctuation taking place over months, or a one-day movement, with the fluctuations taking place over minutes.

From the fractal definition in this example, you can understand why the Elliott wave theory is a perfect example of fractal theory. It postulates that the same pattern—12345ABC—is found in hourly movements as well as movements that last years. Because stock prices are fractal in nature and the Elliott wave theory is the only known fractal theory of stock prices, it should be clear that this theory could be highly significant in helping us interpret market fluctuations. It might allow us to understand, using the modern discoveries of chaos theory, some of the price patterns we have been examining.

FIGURE 6.12   The stock market follows the standard fractal definition in that each small price movement is a part of and a reduced-scale version of the larger price movement.

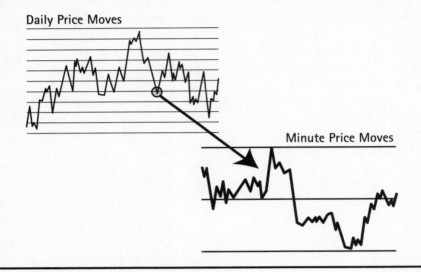

The Elliott wave theory and how the basic 12345ABC pattern builds up and up is one of the best examples of a fractal and the way it is constructed. There are a number of ways to classify fractals, but the classification that is important to us is one that defines in some way the predictability of the geometrical pattern of the fractal. In some fractals,

---

NOTE

Please do not be put off by the discussion of fractals. I have learned over the years that important ideas are usually simple and easy to understand; they are made complex only by people who present them as such. Fractals are truly a simple concept, one that people seem to know instinctively. They are really quite easy to comprehend if approached correctly.

the geometrical pattern is completely random. A random fractal still fits the definition of a fractal: when you take a little part of the whole and blow it up, it does look like the whole, except that with a random fractal there is no way to predict the pattern you will see. Other fractals are not this way. Some are 100% predictable, meaning that when you take a piece of the curve and magnify it, you know exactly what you are going to see. For example, the idealistic Elliott pattern, as we drew it, is 100% predictable; at any point you can predict what you are going to see when you show greater detail.

To help you understand these different kinds of fractals—and ultimately the stock market—I am going to show you two examples of fractals whose underlying patterns have varying degrees of predictability. These two examples are commonly used to illustrate what fractals are.

The first example, the Koch curve, is probably the simplest fractal there is, and the second example, the Mandelbrot curve, is probably the most famous. These examples will prepare us to ask and answer the most important question of all: How predictable is the fractal pattern the stock market makes?

Fractal Example 1: The Koch Curve

To understand the Koch curve, take a straight line and put a little V shape in the middle (Figure 6.13). This V breaks the line into four smaller lines, each equal in length. Do the same with each of these four smaller lines— add a little V to the middle of them. Now there are 16 smaller lines. Add a V to each of these. Do this again and again and again—forever. This is the mathematically infinite but very exact Koch curve. It is a fractal because each part, no matter how small, when magnified, is a scaled-down version of the whole. The Koch curve is interesting because it is mathematically perfect, and it isn't random; you know exactly what you will see and what to expect at each magnification of the curve.

The Elliott wave pattern, as we drew and explained it earlier, is created in a way similar to the Koch curve. The only real difference is that the repeating pattern is a little more complicated. However, the step of repeating a simple action over and over—taking any line and putting five smaller lines in its place—produces an exact pattern similar to the Koch curve.

FIGURE 6.13   The perfectly predictable fractal, the Koch curve, is made by performing a simple procedure over and over. A straight line is broken into four equal lines by putting a V kink in it. You put a V kink into each of these lines, making 16 smaller lines, ad infinitum.

1. Start with a straight line.

2. Put a V kink into it.

3. Then put this basic pattern
   into each straight line.

4. Again...and again....

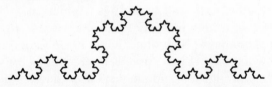

Fractal Example 2: The Mandelbrot Curve

The Mandelbrot curve has patterns that are not quite predictable but similar. Created by the man who discovered fractals, the Mandelbrot curve is the fractal that has come to symbolize not only the entire subject of fractals but also the theory of chaos (Figure 6.14).

FIGURE 6.14   The famous Mandelbrot curve. This fractal pattern has appeared on innumerable book and magazine covers over the years, yet few people know what it is. It comes from a very simple mathematical procedure. In this fractal, all the points in the light area represent one possible answer to that procedure while the black area are those points that represent the other.

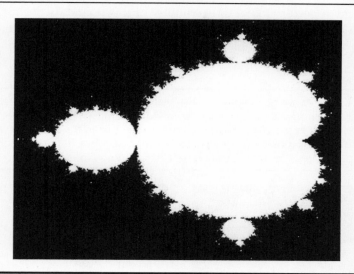

I'm going to show you how the Mandelbrot curve is created by giving you a ridiculously simple analogy. Let's take a circle and paint all the points inside the circle white and all the points outside the circle black. The white points are all the points that satisfy one answer and the black points satisfy the other answer. Answer to what? The answer to this question: How far from the center is each point? Every point painted white is at a location that is less than the radial distance from the center. Every point painted black (everything outside the circle) is at a location that is greater than the radial distance from the center. The circle's circumference is the boundary between these two areas.

This obvious and trivial analogy shows the essence of the simple idea behind the creation of the Mandelbrot curve. Basically, the Mandelbrot curve is a boundary, like the boundary of the circle, that satisfies a similar type of condition. Here, however, the condition is a repeated mathematical calculation that can lead to only two possible results. In the Mandelbrot curve, the white points represent numbers that lead to one result, and the black points represent numbers that lead to the other. In this example, however, the curve or boundary separating the white and black points is not smooth, as the circle is . The curve (if you can call it that) is ragged, with acorn-like shapes sticking out and a bunch of hairy filaments all around it.

To get a better look at the geometry of this boundary, let's magnify it and see what it looks like (Figure 6.15). As we systematically increase the magnification and look deeper and deeper into this boundary, we always find more and more detail. In fact, you never get to a simple,

FIGURE 6.15   As we go deeper into the Mandelbrot curve, we find more and more detail. This fractal never breaks down into a simple pattern or curve. The picture at top right is a magnification of the smaller box in the picture at top left. The middle-left picture is a magnification of the smaller box in the top-right picture, and so on. This magnification process can go on forever.

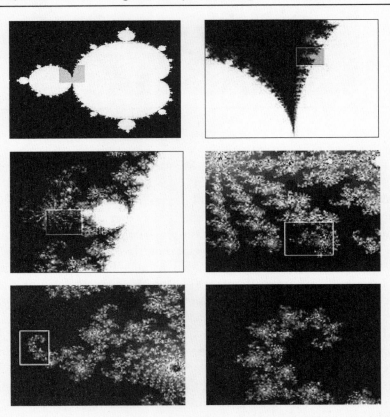

smooth pattern; the greater detail never ends. It is infinite in complexity and never resolves into something simple. The Mandelbrot curve is a wonderful example of a fascinating concept: infinite variation and beauty within a finite boundary.

Can the complicated patterns we see as we magnify the Mandelbrot curve be predicted the way the patterns of the Koch curve can? As far as I know, they cannot. We often see similar patterns as we go deeper into the curve, but I do not believe anyone has developed a way to anticipate exactly what they will see next. There seems to be some symmetry; different forms of what is called the sea horse shape appear repeatedly, but there is also randomness in how that symmetry is displayed. The fractal definition is there, however, since every small section contains all the complexity and variation of pattern that is contained in the whole.

HOW PREDICTABLE IS THE REAL MARKET'S FRACTAL PATTERN?

We saw that the Koch curve is a fractal in which the pattern is predictable. So is the pattern of the idealized Elliott wave pattern. With the Mandelbrot fractal, we saw that the pattern is not identical, but it has similarities or similar repeating patterns that are predictable. There are also fractals that have completely random patterns. All this leads to the $64,000 question: *What type of fractal pattern does the stock market create—100% predictable, somewhat predictable, or random?*

The answer is central to any effort to predict stock prices and to the evaluation of the Elliott wave theory. Is the real stock market, as Elliott wave theorists believe, simply a stretched-out, pushed and pulled version of the idealized Elliott wave pattern in which, if you study it hard enough, you can still see where you are in the pattern and therefore predict what's coming next? Or is it really just a jumble of random zigzag lines?

To understand the question better, let's come back to the Koch curve. We know that the Koch curve is a simple pattern that is 100% predictable; you know exactly what to expect as you magnify it. You can completely predict what you will see. Now let's play a little game.

Suppose, instead of drawing the curve on paper, we actually made it out of thin, malleable wire. We put all those little kinks into the wire, then we take the wire and pull on it a couple of times. What happens to that perfect Koch curve? You should still be able to recognize the resulting curve as the original Koch curve, but pulled and stretched a little.

FIGURE 6.16   If we stretched and pulled the perfect Koch curve, the fractal pattern would no longer be completely predictable. If you stretch it more and more, the pattern eventually becomes completely random, having been transformed from a predictable fractal into a random one. This example suggests an interesting question: Is the real stock market pattern a stretched and pulled Elliott wave pattern but not stretched so much as to be completely random?

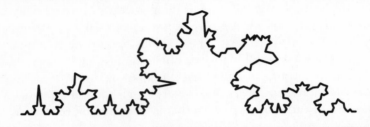

Is the pattern now as predictable as it was originally? Not quite. The basic outline is still predictable, but some of the detail is not.

If you continued to distort the wire more and more, yanking it here and stretching it there, you would eventually lose any resemblance to the original, perfect pattern (Figure 6.16). You would have transformed the perfectly predictable Koch curve into a complex jumble of lines, all of different length and angles and now completely unpredictable.

This is the idea behind the question that we are asking about the Elliott wave pattern. In the real stock market is the basic Elliott wave pattern there, just stretched and pulled a little but with the basic pattern still somewhat recognizable? Or is the stretching and pulling so great that, in practice, the real stock market loses any semblance of that basic ideal pattern?

The Search for Predictability

After 20 years of studying and applying the Elliott wave theory, my experience is that the Elliott wave pattern is sometimes clear and therefore useful for predicting or at least outlining what is coming up. At other times, the pattern of the market is so completely random that no Elliott wave pattern can be discerned. At these times, the market is completely unpredictable using the Elliott wave theory. Therefore, *sometimes the Elliott wave fractal pattern is discernible, making the market somewhat predictable, and at other times, it is random.* This observation aligns with the conclusion of the basic model introduced in Chapter 2.

Elliott wave theorists often say that this is wrong and that the complete pattern is almost always clearly there. In general, they are right; the study of past markets almost always shows the market making a completed pattern. However, they always do this analysis after the fact. When you have to make real-time, day-to-day decisions, there are just too many points along the way where you could have said a movement was complete when it really wasn't. The rules and exceptions are so broad and so many variations are allowed that we often don't know what to project. So yes, after the fact one can look back and say, "See, here it is"; but in practice, it isn't this way.

The record of people using the Elliott wave theory over the years generally demonstrates partial predictability. Although there have been many startling successes, there have also been many failures. In practice, there always seems to be an alternate wave count, which indicates that the Elliott wave theory, by itself, is somewhat incomplete.

It is interesting that neither the Elliott wave theorists nor those critical of the theory address this important question in any depth. Both believers in and critics of the theory see it as being either 100% right or 100% wrong. This is unfortunate because the Elliott wave theory does not, by its nature, lie at either of these two extremes. Efforts to make it a perfect theory actually destroy its value, and efforts to deny it ignore the new discoveries made in chaos theory.

The idea that the Elliott wave theory is not complete on its own does not invalidate the theory or make it wrong. It just reflects what I believe is the actual situation—that the market is sometimes predictable and sometimes random.

Nevertheless, even with this limitation, there is no better way to try to map the market. If you have to forecast how prices will probably unfold, there is no better starting point than the basic Elliott wave fractal pattern. This is especially true when you add to the Elliott wave theory the information presented in the first five chapters of this book. With these other tools, it often becomes possible to overcome many of the uncertainties in the Elliott wave pattern.

Applying the Elliott Wave Theory

How do you actually make the Elliott wave theory work? As I have said, the Elliott wave theory presents the pattern or map against which you evaluate the actual pattern of the real market. It is a constant, ongoing activity and one that needs to remain flexible so you can change your mind freely if warranted. I use the tools described in the previous chapters to help me estimate where in the wave count the stock market is, but wide allowances are made for the Elliott wave variations I mentioned earlier.

I usually start at a major market bottom or other relative point of certainty. Then, I make every effort to determine where that point is in the Elliott wave count. I study both daily and weekly charts of the major indexes to help me find the count. I use the S&P 500, the Dow Jones industrials, the Russell 2000, the NASDAQ Composite Index, and a high-tech index, because sometimes the count is clearer on one index than it is on another. I have found that the Elliott wave count is clearest during volatile markets—when feedback loops are functioning—and that dull markets with low volatility usually produce random and confusing patterns.

NOTE

Don't force the count. If you don't know, you don't know. Remember that there will be times when the pattern is incomprehensible and prediction impossible. Learn to live with that; you must become used to not knowing. Because of this, be suspicious of anyone who always has an opinion. People who always have an opinion are either fooling themselves or selling something.

No matter how impatient you get while waiting to identify exactly where the wave count is, you must fight the tendency of always having to know. This is very important. I have learned that the market will always show what it is doing if you have patience. You have to be willing to say, "I don't know," and then wait until you see something that you can clearly identify. Remember, there are many times when the market is random and unpredictable—in fact, it's like that most of the time.

Accurate Prediction Takes Vigilance

You might think that after 30 years I would have become more certain in the art of stock prediction, but this is not what has happened; I have become more humble. I originally thought that the fundamentals of the market stayed the same, that behind the ever-changing economic picture, a few things remained constant. After all, there are always buyers and sellers and the market either goes up or down. I still believe that, but much less so.

Be Wary of Doomsayers

The Elliott wave theory should never be used to predict major crashes or calamities in the future, and prognosticators who do this only contribute to the invalidation of a very useful theory. When you are pretty certain the stock market has completed a major 12345 movement, all you know is that the market is probably headed for an ABC correction. It could be a crash, but it is just as likely to be an irregular correction in which, after a very mild wave A, the wave B will carry prices to new highs for a number of years. The Elliott wave theory alone cannot predict what form the ABC correction will take. You must include other factors to help you decide what type of top it is going to be.

The activity of stock market speculation takes intense and persistent study, and you must be open to the study of something that is evolving and changing. People do learn. Investors know a lot more about stocks than their forbears. The professors have pushed forward our understanding of investment markets, and we now have a firmer theoretical foundation. Investors therefore react differently than they used to.

I have methodically covered all the information that I believe is necessary to understand most stock markets and to condition the reader to expect a new market environment. It is now time to show how I apply such knowledge in the real world—to the stock market at the end of 2001. The theories I used to do this are the same ones I used to predict the end of the 1982–2000 bull market in my first book, *A Strategic Guide to the Coming Roller-Coaster Market*. This time, however, I'll apply them to help determine the structure and form of the expected trading range market, how long it will last, and how low and high it will range. The Elliott wave theory is used to forecast the basic form for this trading range. Finally, in Chapter 8, strategies are offered that might do well during this forecasted period.

7

Trading
Range Markets

THE CORRECTION: WHAT WILL IT LOOK LIKE?

As we saw in the last chapter, the most complicated part of Elliott wave theory is the corrective waves. More variations of pattern are allowed for corrective waves than for any other wave types. Basically, a correction is a halt in the primary trend of the market. It can manifest either by prices declining or by prices marking time by moving up and down in a sideways pattern. It is our business now to investigate and consider the most likely form and type of correction and how to possibly profit from it.

Past Trading Range Markets

There is a long history of the stock market entering into extended trading ranges, periods where prices moved up and down in large bull and bear markets but made little forward progress. In fact, since 1900, stock prices were in essentially long-term trading ranges more than 50% of the time. I calculate that we have had three such periods since 1900.

   The first period occurred right after the turn of the century (a hundred years ago) and lasted about 15 years. It started with the Dow Jones industrials making an all-time high of 75.57 on January 19, 1906. From that lofty peak it declined 48% over almost two years, hitting bottom on November 15, 1907, at 38.88. Within two years it had recovered almost the entire previous decline, reaching a second peak at 73.76 on November 19, 1909. The cheer was short-lived, however, as the market then slid slowly toward bottom almost two years later, at 53.51, on September 1, 1911.

For the next three years, prices were completely lifeless. From that September low, prices worked their way up to a local high of 69.08 on September 30, 1912, then eroded back down to a second bottom on July 30, 1914, at 52.40. Prices then came back to life. They rallied strongly to a new all-time high of 110.15, a gain of 110% over two and a half years, hitting the peak price on November 21, 1916. The cheer was again short-lived as prices declined in one year to 65.95, hitting bottom on December 19, 1917. Another two-year bull market followed, with prices rising slightly above the previous peak, getting to 119.62 on November 3, 1919. This was again followed by a bear market, which hit a low of 63.90 on August 21, 1921. From the 1906 high of 75.57 to the low in 1921 of 63.90, prices had effectively gone nowhere.

The second trading range period started in 1937 after a five-year rally recovered some of the collapsed prices of the Great Crash. From a high of 195.59 on March 10, 1937, the market declined to a low of 97.46 almost exactly one year later, on March 31, 1938. From that low it quickly recovered to 158.90 by November 10, 1938, only to again go into a long, slow decline over four years back to 92.69, hitting bottom on April 28, 1942. A four-year bull market ensued, hitting a high of 213.36 on May 29, 1946. For the next three years, prices went into a dead period, first hitting a low of 160.49 on October 30, 1946, followed by a high of 194.49 on June 14, 1948, and then another low of 160.62 on June 14, 1949. Over the 12 years between 1937 to 1949, prices effectively went nowhere.

The third trading range period was the 16 years between 1966 and 1982. The Dow industrials hit 1,000 in 1966 and didn't effectively break above it until 1982. The next chapter goes into the details of this period.

"Normalized" Thinking

I remember as a child sitting with my parents and their friends one evening when my father posed a question that everyone, including me, failed to answer correctly. He asked: "If a car goes a half a mile at 30 miles an hour, how fast does it have to go the second half-mile to average 60 miles an hour for the whole mile?" After a lot of arguing, we all agreed that it had to be 90 miles an hour. My father laughed at us and said, "No. In fact it can't be done. Sixty miles an hour is a mile a minute. The car has already used up a minute traveling the first half-mile at 30 miles an hour. To average 60 miles an hour the car would have to traverse the final half-mile in zero time. It would have to go at an infinite speed." I couldn't accept his reasoning and I embarrassed myself by arguing for half the night that 90 miles an hour would still do the trick, but he was right.

This story leads us into a less complicated but similar question regarding stock prices. The question is this. The long-term average gain in stocks (the S&P 500) since 1928 is just about 10.5%. Over the last 20 years, the S&P 500 has averaged a gain of approximately 16% per year. Let me ask a similar question: If the stock market has averaged 16% per year for the last 20 years, what does it have to earn over the next 20 years to average 10.5% over the full 40 years? Here, it is allowable to do the simple calculation I had used that didn't work with my father's question. If we do the simple calculation, the market has to average 5% return per year over the next 20 years to come in at its long-term average.

Figure 7.1 dramatizes the idea behind this question by charting the price of the S&P 500 since 1940. The trendline in the graph, drawn

---

FIGURE 7.1   The stock market has gotten far ahead of its 70-year growth rate. It would be normal to adjust by going through a time correction, that is, marking time by making little price progress. What would look like a sideways move on this long-term price chart, however, would really be composed of rather lengthy bull and bear markets.

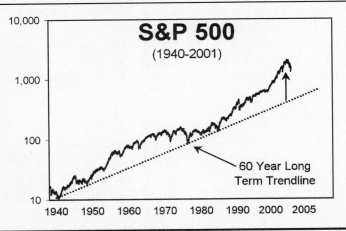

against the bottom of the market after the Great Crash (not shown), rises at about 7% per year. When you include the reinvestment of dividends of approximately 3.5% per year, this line represents a total return from stocks (growth plus dividends) of 10.5%.

From a certain perspective, what has happened in the market since March 2000 can be seen as natural. Investing is always a two-sided proposition. In March 1982, I gave a talk on the long-term future of the stock market. I said that every generation usually has the opportunity to experience the fantastic potential of stock investing, then gets carried away, overspeculates, and learns firsthand the negative side of stock investing. I said that this baby boom generation would probably be given the same opportunity. I believe the first part of this learning cycle is now complete. It is time for the baby boom generation to learn firsthand, just as their parents did, the difficulties of stock investing, and then their investment education will be complete. The major lessons to be learned are these.

- Wealth comes with great difficulty and to only a few.
- There is no magic formula; making money in the stock market requires constant vigilance and training.
- When the future looks bright and everything seems too good, it probably is. Similarly, when the future seems very bleak and everything too bad, it also probably isn't.

THE CURRENT ELLIOTT WAVE PATTERN

As I explained in Chapter 6, if you want to outline the future pattern for stock prices, there is no better template to lay down than the Elliott wave pattern. Many investors and analysts might disagree with me on this point since the Elliott wave pattern doesn't consider or address any economic factors in its formulation and, as we've said, the long-term movement of prices is caused by economics. That said, I still say there is still no better tool to use when projecting the future course of stock prices than a basic Elliott wave pattern. The theory works because it permits enough variation and stretching to allow for a number of different economic scenarios. For example, I might predict that a market advance will occur in two thrusting waves or sections, but there is no way to know their size or duration; that would depend on the unfolding economic situation. The basic pattern of two waves, however, should manifest—not three or four. This is all the projection intends to do—produce a broad outline of what to expect.

When you use the Elliott wave theory, you must understand that any pattern projected must remain fluid. The number of Elliott wave variations demands that any pattern projection must be fluid and adjusted as the real pattern unfolds over time. It is just a broad guideline to project with.

Let's begin by trying to determine how the Elliott wave count stands now. You should always start from some point of high certainty. The point of certainty I use is the 1982 bottom, which ended the 16-year correction and began, in my opinion, the long bull market we have been in. Figure 7.2 shows the S&P 500 since 1980, and I've indicated on the chart what I think the count is.

The long bull market has been in play off the 1982 bottom now for close to 20 years. I read the first movement from 1982 to 1984, which fi-

FIGURE 7.2   The hypothetical Elliott wave count on the market as of 2001. These counts must always remain fluid. The count shown indicates that the market seems to have started into a major, wave 4 correction. I project that wave 4 will be lengthy, forming an extended trading range. A final fifth wave (which I call the final stampede) should follow once wave 4 completes.

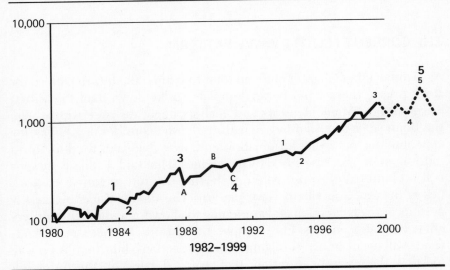

153

nally broke through the Dow 1,000 barrier, as the first advancing wave (wave 1). Wave 2 was the short, six-month correction through the summer of 1984. Wave 3 carried all the way to the top of 1987, just before the crash. Wave 4 was not the 1987 crash—the 1987 crash started wave 4. The 1987 crash was the first wave down (the A wave) of a longer-term ABC correction, as shown in Figure 7.2. I believe the C wave of this wave 4 finishes with the recession of 1990.

Wave 5 has been in play since 1990; it is an extension. Wave 1 of this fifth wave is the movement from 1990 to 1993. Wave 2 is simple and is the correction of 1994. Wave 3 started in 1994, carried on for 6 years, and had extensions of its own. It finished in 2000. Since 2000, the market entered into the fourth-wave correction of the final fifth wave.

The Fourth Wave

The stock market has started into a major fourth-wave correction. Although the Elliott wave theory does not directly detail the time length of its waves (only their patterns), it does address the time length of some movements under certain situations, particularly wave 4 corrections.

One Elliott wave principle that gives some guidance concerning time is called the rule of alternation. The *rule of alternation* addresses the correction waves, waves 2 and 4: If wave 2 is simple, wave 4 will be complex or vice versa. In our case, the 1994 wave 2 was very simple. Wave 3 was the extension move from 1994 to 2000. The rule of alternation implies that wave 4 should probably be complex—composed of a number of movements and stretched out in time. I believe that wave 4 will be a special type of correction, which Elliott and other wave theorists call a horizontal triangular correction.

R.N. Elliott, in one of his *Financial World* articles, said the following about horizontal triangular corrections: "Triangular corrections are protracted trend hesitations. The main movement may have gone too far and too fast in relation to the slower economic processes, and prices proceed to mark time until the underlying forces catch up."

In a sense this Elliott wave interpretation is just telling us what we already know about the market, that it has gone through a huge run-up for a long time without any extended correction. The stock market boom was accompanied by constantly increasing public participation in stock investing, ultimately culminating in broad technology and Internet speculation of 1998 to 2000. The point emphasized here is that Elliott wave

FIGURE 7.3   R.N. Elliott's drawing of a fourth wave horizontal triangular correction. Notice that the wave 2 correction is small, so that the whole advance has been a very rapid 123. The market has gotten ahead of itself and now experiences a special type of correction beyond the normal ABC type. The horizontal correction has five movements in it instead of the normal three (the ABC), which lengthens the correction. You can see from the shape of the waves that if the correction lasted long enough it would form a long trading range market.

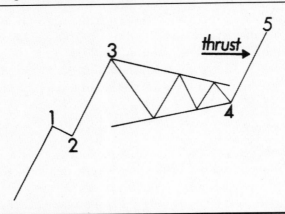

theory allows for this type of situation by detailing a special type of correction that could follow—a wave 4, horizontal triangular correction. Figure 7.3 shows this type of correction, as taken from Elliott's original diagrams.

The Internal Structure of the Fourth Wave

The basic projection is that the market made a major top in 2000 as originally forecasted and has started in on an extended fourth wave correction. That correction will probably be a horizontal triangular correction, with the movements forming the correction being the market swings that make up the trading range market.

Figure 7.4 shows some of the smaller waves in a fourth wave horizontal triangular correction. As already noted, the whole correction is composed of five movements. In my opinion, two or three of these movements will be large enough to be classified as bull or bear markets in their own right. As diagrammed, in a horizontal triangle each one of the five movements breaks down into three smaller movements (ABC-type movements).

FIGURE 7.4.   The internal structure of a horizontal triangular correction as Elliott drew it. Even though it is considered a correction, if each of these movements (1, 2, 3, 4, and 5) is large and long enough, they could be considered bull and bear markets in their own right. Notice that each of the five movements of the correction break down into three submovements of smaller degree.

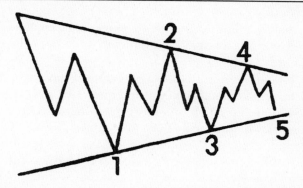

If this is the projection, then each sell-off (waves 1, 3, and 5) should break down into two distinct submovements. Likewise, each of the rallies (2 and 4) should break down into two distinct advancing waves. If only one advancing or declining wave is visible and obvious, then that wave is not complete—more is to follow. Of course, certain cutoffs have to be established because this is just a projection; it must remain fluid. Just because I'm expecting a horizontal correction doesn't mean that the market will produce it. Many other patterns and forms of corrections can happen, but of all of them, the horizontal correction seems the most likely.

Contracting Volatility

In Figure 7.4, notice that as the horizontal triangle forms, the up-and-down movements become smaller and smaller. In other words, the triangle becomes narrower as we move to the right. This points to another reason I'm expecting that the correction will be of this form: market volatility. It has been my experience, that after a speculative run-up like we saw in the market from 1998 to 2000, with the bubble bursting in the technology and Internet sectors, it is usual for stock prices starting with high volatility to end a movement with very low volatility.

Volatility is a measure of how much prices move up and down—whether they are active or muted. In the two years between 1998 and 2000, the market manifested (as measured by the Nasdaq composite) a very high level of volatility, with record percentage changes for the advance immediately followed by record percentage changes in the decline. In a sense it was a huge index blow-off—the opposite of a selling climax.

Do you remember our discussion of technical analysis and how a climax ends? Prices fall on huge volume and then reverse very quickly, rising on huge volume. This high volatility is soon followed by a market that begins to quiet down, eventually becoming almost lifeless. The opposite of that, huge index blow-off, would produce the same phenomenon, except in reverse. The market would go up, with high volatility, but then quickly reverse in a large market sell-off. Volatility would remain high for a while, but slowly, after the first sell-off, the subsequent price motion would slowly die down as the correction carried forward and stabilized. Figure 7.5 shows such a market trend.

Once the correction has run its course and the volatility dies, the market should begin an advance to new highs. Theoretically, the blow-off is not the end of the whole move but a huge thrust that needs a major correction before prices can resume their upward march.

What all this means is that in the near future the stock market should become very boring. I don't like to put it that way, but there really is no other way to say it. During this period, investors will start looking around for alternative strategies in an effort to continue to increase their money. It is during this boring period that smart investors should start getting themselves ready for the final stampede—the final wave 5.

The Time Scale of the Trading Range Period

Figure 7.5 displays a schematic of the decreasing volatility that I'm expecting in the market. It should be a market where most investors become bored and disenchanted with stocks. They will be hoping for a return of the good old speculative days, but that won't happen. They will look for excitement and get inactivity. How long should this trading range market last? This is a very difficult question to answer.

In January 2000, I projected that the trading range would last from two to four years. Back then, however, the correction hadn't even started

FIGURE 7.5 A schematic of the type of market to expect from the Nasdaq composite if it goes through a horizontal correction. As it is forming such a pattern, the volatility of prices should contract like the coiling of a spring.

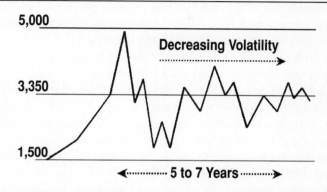

yet, so it was difficult to formulate a reliable answer to the how-long question since the way the correction would unfold was much less clear. Now that a major correction seems to have started, the form of the correction is easier to see and a time length easier to predict. A possible guide is provided by considering the first 6 years of the 16-year (1966 to 1982), trading range market.

The long post-WWII bull market started in 1949, going all the way to 1968 where it ended in a speculative flurry similar to but much less intense than the recent one. A number of indexes showed that the subsequent correction starting in 1968 carried forward for six years, ending in 1974. Therefore, I think that a reasonable projection for the length of the coming trading range market is 5 to 7 years. It would be normal for a trading range market of 5 to 7 years to follow a long bull market that has lasted, by many accounts, 18 years.

THE ECONOMIC "WHY"

In the model presented in Chapter 2, the long-term movement in stock prices should reflect the changing economic picture. There is the fair-value term that depends only on fundamentals—dividends and interest rates. It is only during price movements that last less than 9 months that technical considerations and market instabilities can dominate and the economic picture be set aside. If a trading range market is to last from 5 to 7 years, there must be an economic reason for it, an economic or investment story behind such an occurrence.

Simply put, the stock market has gotten way ahead of itself in its speculation phase, and the implied economic growth that these high prices require will not be realized during the next 10 years. We will have economic growth, but it will be far less than is implied by current prices. Let's look at current prices and what they imply.

To start, let's see what our stacking-the-money theory for fair value can illuminate. Consider an important financial ratio, the *dividend yield for stocks*, which is calculated by dividing dividends from the last 12 months by price. The result is the yield on stocks, a comparable financial number in the stock market to yields on bonds. As shown in Figure 7.6, the current dividend rate on the S&P 500 is 1.3%—the lowest reading in history. But what does this dividend yield for stocks mean?

Figure 7.7 is from chapter 3, where this idea was more fully explained. It shows, using the fair-value theory of stacking the money, how and why a low dividend yield (or the same thing—a high PE ratio) implies that Wall Street is expecting very high levels of growth in earnings and dividends.

The low dividend yields result because the present dividend is tiny compared to the high stack (price) of all those huge expected dividends. In other words, the current price of stocks is built on a very high—in fact, a record high—expectation of earnings and dividends growth. If this growth doesn't materialize, we will know that current prices were too high and the expectations too extreme, and a major readjustment will occur.

We can do a very quick calculation to see what the current PE ratio of the S&P 500 is implying as far as expected earnings and dividend growth. In December 2001, the PE ratio of the S&P 500 was 31. The 10-year treasury interest rate is 5%. From a well-known formula based on stacking the money, the current price of the S&P 500 is therefore implying an expected growth rate of 13% per year over the next 7 to 10 years. If growth comes in at this high rate, stocks will have been fairly priced. Thirteen percent is a pretty high rate of growth to achieve.

Let's be very clear: We can have very good continued earnings and dividend growth and still have a major market adjustment. Current prices allow for almost no disappointment of any kind, and if anything

FIGURE 7.6 Current dividend rates on the S&P 500. At any given moment, the dividend yield represents Wall Street's expectations for earnings and dividend growth. The current ratio implies the highest expected growth in earnings and dividends in many years.

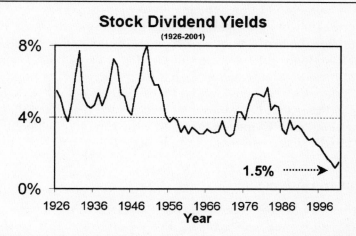

FIGURE 7.7 A low dividend yield implies that Wall Street is expecting high dividend (and earnings) growth in the future. The expectation of future growth allows investors to accept the low dividend yield today. If confidence in the expected growth were ever shaken, a major price readjustment would occur.

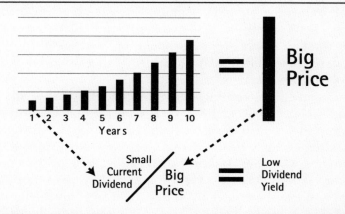

less than record-breaking numbers appear, there will be disappointment. In the speculative phase of the market, prices got ahead of themselves, and sooner or later, we must pay the piper. Growth can occur for only so long and expectations can rise to the moon, but eventually the price of stock must be rooted in a fundamental basis (namely, D/I).

Unfortunately, it always takes a while for investors to finally recognize that this is the new economic paradigm. It's not as if someone rings a bell and suddenly everyone recognizes what is happening. Usually, a consistent erosion of expectation dashes the resurgences of hope along the way. When that happens enough times, there is a sudden change in thinking and reluctant but widespread acceptance that a less-than-rosy period has emerged. In today's market, by the time that happens, we'll be well into the major correction I'm predicting.

Overvalued, Undervalued

One of the errors I hear continually on Wall Street is the misuse of the terms *overvalued* and *undervalued*. People often say that stocks are overvalued or undervalued. When asked why they have that opinion, they usually refer to some ratio based on either the PE ratio or the dividend yield. I have no argument with looking at these ratios, but I do have a quarrel with associating these ratios with the terms *overvalued* and *undervalued*.

For one thing, these are very powerful words. The word *overvalued* implies that the current price of a stock is higher than its true worth. No one wants to be a sucker and pay more than something is worth, yet no one really knows exactly what something is worth. These ratios do not measure whether stocks are undervalued or overvalued; the PE ratio and dividend yields measure Wall Street's expectation for the future growth of earnings and dividends.

For example, a record high PE ratio (low dividend yield) doesn't mean that stocks are overvalued. It only means that Wall Street's expectation for the growth of earnings and dividends over the next 5 or 6 years is extremely high. If, after 5 years, earnings and dividends do grow at the implied rate, then and only then can we look back and say that prices were fairly valued. If over the next 5 years, earnings and dividends grow at less than the implied rate, then and only then can we say that prices were overvalued. Only if earnings and dividends grow at more than the implied rate can we look back and say that prices were actually undervalued.

I think we will find during the next 6 years that the earnings and dividends that this American economy can produce will grow at a lower rate than prices are implying (through their dividend yields and PE ratios). That will be the reason the market ultimately forms and experiences a trading range market. In hindsight it will become clear that stock prices just got too far ahead of themselves during the speculative phase of an investment cycle.

THE FINAL STAMPEDE

A careful look at Figure 7.2 shows that, according to my interpretation of the Elliott wave count, a final fifth advancing wave should follow the fourth wave (trading range) correction. This fifth wave should not be a minor Elliott wave movement but a bull market of considerable proportions. Since it is theoretically the final wave of the movement that started in 1982, I call it the final stampede.

At this time there is no way of using the Elliott wave theory to make a realistic projection about its character or nature. The only relevant comment concerning the character and form of a fifth wave movement that follows a horizontal correction is the following quote from *The Works of R.N. Elliott*.

> At the conclusion of a horizontal triangle, the market will resume the trend that was interrupted by the triangle, and the direction of that trend will be the same as that of triangular wave 2. The "break-out" from the horizontal triangle (in the direction of triangular wave 2) will usually be fast and represent the final wave of the main movement, and be followed by reversal of the trend. The extent of the "break-out" will usually approximate the distance between the widest parts of the triangle. The diagrams [shown here] illustrate the "break-out" from horizontal triangles.

Therefore, according to Elliott, once the horizontal correction is over, the subsequent breakout (the final fifth wave) should be very fast. It also should go to new high prices, above previous highs, equal to the size of the price range during the correction.

I honestly don't give much credence to a projection like this. For me it is too far out and too theoretical; it isn't yet clear that the correction will be a horizontal one! The final fifth wave could be as short as 3 years or as long as 10. The economic picture will have to be considered very carefully at that time to evaluate what form and structure the final fifth wave may take, but that is a problem for a later day.

8

Trading Range Investment Strategies

This chapter focuses on strategies intended primarily for an extended trading range market.

Caution

We will now look at several investment strategies based on backtesting, that is, taking historical numbers and testing how a contemporary strategy would have done in the past. In back-testing a strategy, you assume that today's investment vehicles were available in the past and that the results of these studies were possible. For the purpose of the study, I assumed that we could have used the same index mutual funds, spiders, and today's low commissions and narrow spreads (the difference between the bid and ask price), even though they were not available then. There is no implication that anyone actually achieved these results or could have during the period of the study, these are simply theoretical calculations based on certain assumptions. The hope is that if these strategies might have produced a positive result during the last sideways period, they may be useful in the next.

As I've already indicated, in coming years I'm expecting bull markets lasting from 1 to 2 years and encompassing 30% to 40% rises; these will be followed by bear markets lasting 9 months to a year and declining from 20% to 25%. There will be considerable up-and-down motion but little overall gain. It might seem strange to try to earn superior returns if stock prices are essentially in a back-and-forth trading range. One obvious strategy is to try to buy at the bottom of the range and sell near the top, but this, of course, depends on whether an investor can actually do this.

The last time the market experienced a long sideways trading range was from 1966 to 1982. The Dow Jones industrials hit 1,000 in 1966 and bounced between 700 and 1,000, making little progress for 16 years. Although I'm not expecting a sideways market so severe, this often-ignored period can provide us with fertile ground for testing various strategies that might work well during another trading range market.

No two markets are ever the same. We will assume, however, that the three feedback loops in the stock market model have created many recurring patterns and events over many market cycles. These similar patterns might show up and be measurable if the market is approached and studied in certain ways. This means that, although the economic picture is not anything like the 1970s, the forces that drive the feedback loops—human emotion and reaction—are still the same today as they were back then. We are looking for how this similarity manifests in stock price movements. This chapter presents strategies, back-tested from 1966 to 1982, that may be useful in the future.

TWO APPROACHES TO MARKET TIMING

There are two general approaches to market timing (Figure 8.1). The first approach tries to find the exact top or bottom of a price movement. It employs contrary opinion, interest rates, divergences, sector analysis, and price patterns to pinpoint the market top and bottom as closely as possible, though reaching the Holy Grail of consistently finding the exact top or bottom is obviously very difficult.

The second approach to market timing doesn't try to find tops or bottoms, but instead attempts to locate the moment when a new price trend has established itself. It uses indicators that give signals *after* a top or bottom has been made. The idea is to let the market make top or bottom

FIGURE 8.1   There are two categories of market indicators, defined by what the indicator is intending to accomplish. Some indicators try to locate exact tops and bottoms. The others try to identify and confirm a new price trend. When used in the same time domain, these two categories almost always contradict each other.

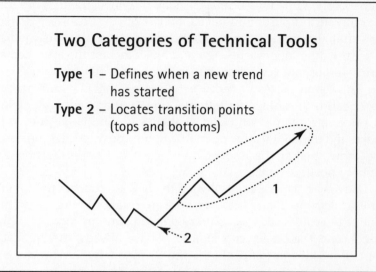

Two Categories of Technical Tools

Type 1 – Defines when a new trend
has started
Type 2 – Locates transition points
(tops and bottoms)

and then look for indications that the market has started a new price trend.

You can usually classify an indicator into one of these two approaches. The first approach truly tries to predict the future. The final result is something like, "The indicators strongly predict that the market will stop going down now and start going up." The second approach, rather than being predictive, confirms that a move has begun. Quite often, this confirming approach is characterized by the measurement of a cutoff, meaning that prices have gone to a certain point that now proves the trend has reversed and conditions have changed. This type of indicator could be a major price index breaking a trendline, the confirmation of two important indices breaking two similar trendlines, prices rising above an established fixed percent, or a moving average turning up or down.

The Strongest Market Signal

The two approaches to market timing—**predictive** and **confirming**—almost always give conflicting signals when analyzing movements of the same time domain. That is okay because they are used for different purposes and have different goals. If contrary opinion says that the market has reached bottom over the intermediate term, the other approach—trending indicators for the intermediate term—almost always indicates that the trend is still down.

This is normal. Why? Because it is normal that investors become very bearish (furnishing us with buy signals using contrary opinion) as prices are plummeting and at their low. The large price drop makes the trend indicators point down, but the predictive indicators are showing that the end of the decline has been reached and higher prices are ahead.

However, there are times when the two approaches do not give conflicting signals, and these are very important to note. When predictive indicators such as contrary opinion strongly indicate higher prices, and the confirming indicators have already confirmed the start of a slight uptrend, that is the strongest buy signal there is. There is nothing more reliable or important than when this unusual situation happens.

Why is this so? It is expected that, as prices move up, more and more investors will become bullish. When, however, the bearish sentiment stays high or even moves higher as prices also move higher, that is not expected, and so it is the sign of a very strong stock market. At these moments, what is happening is that no one believes the upward price movement is real or that it will last. This skepticism is the fuel needed to keep the movement going, usually for some time.

The same holds true when both categories of indicators are confirming that prices are declining. If contrary opinion is extremely bullish and stock prices have already started down, so much so that trend-following indicators are confirming the downtrend, there is no more reliable or important sell indicator.

For example, back in the 1970s and early 1980s, the most reliable confirmation of a new upward trend was when the advance-decline line rallied very strongly for 10 days. Here is what would happen: The market would look extremely weak after going through an intermediate decline. Then, seemingly out of nowhere and for no apparent reason, prices would stage a violent rally. The rally would go straight up for about 10 days with phenomenal breadth. Many investors, caught off guard and seeing the market apparently getting overbought, would wait for a pullback to buy. But the pullback seldom came. When this situation occurred, the best strategy was to simply buy into the overbought market, assuming that the rally was so strong any sell-off would be mild and temporary and the move would immediately carry forward. This strong initial showing in the advance-decline line was almost always confirmation that the bottom had been made and that a new uptrend—likely to last for at least 6 months—had been established.

There are three reasons that market technicians often espouse different opinions about the market. The first is that one technician is looking for an exact top and bottom while another is looking at the market trend. The second is that they may be talking about two different time domains, as mentioned in Chapter 2; the short-term trend may be up while the long-term trend is down. The third reason is simply that they may truly have different opinions.

Which Approach Is Best?

I personally prefer the approach of the predicting indicators; I like the challenge it presents and it suits my personality better. In truth, however, both predicting and confirming indicators are needed, and they are equally important. Let me show you why. Suppose that predictive indicators strongly show that the market is ready to start a major uptrend in prices. As an investor, you can do two things. One is to take a position in a broad-based index and wait to see if the movement starts. If it does, you will have bought near the lows. Your second possible action is to wait for prices to actually start rising and for some event to confirm the trend; then you would buy into the broad-based index, expecting that the trend—already confirmed—would continue. Some analysts call this the "trend is now your friend" approach.

Either way works, as it happens, and I use one or the other, depending on how I feel about the market and other factors. The choice depends on how close to a pivotal point you are and how reliable you feel that pivotal point is (explained in an earlier chapter).

Interestingly, even if you use the first method, you will still need the second category of indicators eventually. Let me explain. Suppose the predictive indicators are saying the market is ready for a good long advance. You purchase a broad-based index based on this expectation, and the move begins. The predictive indicators, however, do not always tell you what sectors of the market will be the best performers during the up move. This is especially true as the move matures. As the move progresses, it is noted that a certain class of stocks is far outperforming another class. This type of information comes from the second, trend-confirming class of indicators. In practice, you take an initial position in a broad-based index using the predictive indicators, but as the move unfolds you adjust the investment using trend-type indicators to find better-performing broad-based sectors.

The studies I did for this book used indicators from the second category—indicators that define market price trends. I chose them because they are much easier to back-test than predictive indicators. Trend-confirming indicators are usually very exact and mathematical, so it is easy to define exact points where the trend is either up or down.

The simplest example of a confirming-type indicator is when prices break through a trendline. But how and where to draw a trendline to do a study is very subjective. We get around that by using another technical tool, the moving average, to establish an objective way of drawing trend-lines. From this point forward, the studies in this chapter all use moving averages in one way or another.

Market Timing Using Moving Averages

Moving-average trend indicators are part of the second approach to market timing—they provide a mathematical technique useful in defining market trends. To create a moving average, you add up the price of an index for a specific number of days and divide the sum by the number of days. We call the result a moving average because it moves in time and changes with the addition of each new day. A moving average is like a time window that shows you the latest average price over the time specified.

Here is an example. To create a moving average, consider any time period—for example, 23 days—and then calculate the average price of a stock or market index over that period. The average price *moves*, or changes, a little every day because the time period (in this example, the last 23 days) is always changing. You have to recalculate the average every day. Figure 8.2 shows a 23-day moving average of the S&P 500 over the 18-month period between 1/31/97 and 7/31/98.

FIGURE 8.2   Example of a moving average. Notice how the moving average (*dotted line*) smoothes out price fluctuations and lags behind the most recent price.

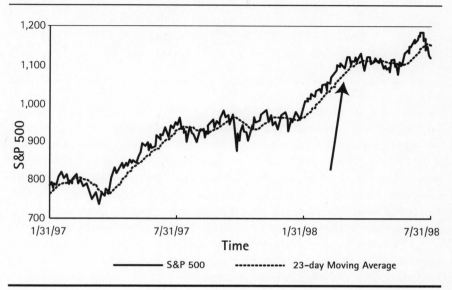

A moving average has the effect of smoothing out the price fluctuations that occur within the time frame of the average. In our example of a 23-day moving average, a sharp movement over 2 days will be softened because you're averaging those 2 days against the other 21 days. Similarly, if you had a 200-day moving average, a sharp movement that occurred over 2 or 3 weeks would be blended away by all the other days in the average. Moving averages act as filters; they help filter out the price movements that occur over shorter periods within the *overall* period being measured.

After you calculate a moving average, there are a number of ways to use it to define market trends. The method that many technicians use and the one I used in these studies is shown in the sidebar. Longer-term moving averages are sensitive to long-term price trends, and shorter-term moving averages react to and show short-term price trends.

> ## Defining Trends Using Moving Averages
>
> The moving average is used as a cutoff to define a trend. If the last price of an index raises its average price for that index, the trend for prices is considered up. Similarly, the trend of prices is considered down when the current price is below the moving average.

Moving averages always measure where prices have already been, lagging behind the most recent changes in price, which is exactly what we want. Remember that a moving average won't help you predict—it is a mathematical measure to establish a running cutoff number to define something. In an advancing market, the most recent prices will eventually cross over and be above the moving average, constantly signaling that the trend is up, whereas in a declining market, prices will cross over and be below the moving average, signaling that the trend is down.

All of which leaves one very important question unanswered: If we're going to use a moving average to define the market trend, what time period should the moving average measure?

MY FIRST MOVING-AVERAGE STUDY

Through the years, I have watched as various market advisors used different moving averages in their work. Some used a 200-day average to detect long-term trends. Others used a 39-week (195-day) average. Some used a 100-day average to find intermediate-term trends, and others used 10-, 25-, 50-, or 75-day averages. Nowhere did I see an explanation of why they chose these time periods. It seemed suspicious that they always used numbers that ended in 10s or 5s (e.g., 10, 20, 25, 50, 100, 195, or 200). Why not 73 days, for example? Where was a study that showed which moving averages worked best at finding the different market trends? I saw small studies, but none that I thought was convincing.

To answer this question I set out in 1983 to backtest every moving average from 5-day to 200-day averages. My goal was to find which moving averages produced the best return over a long period. I also had another motive: I realized that the moving-average study might also allow me to test the long-held belief that the stock market might be following certain natural time cycles.

Time Cycles in the Market

For many years people have believed that the stock market might operate according to certain repetitive time cycles. For example, in the 1950s, 1960s, and 1970s, there was widespread belief and talk of the $4\frac{1}{3}$-year business and investment cycle. Major market bottoms often occurred about $4\frac{1}{3}$ years apart. Figure 8.3 illustrates the popular $4\frac{1}{3}$-year market cycle, and I think it is obvious from it why belief in the $4\frac{1}{3}$-year cycle became widely accepted.

Repetitious time cycles of other frequencies also seemed to occur, and analysts made some effort to identify them, too. One of the original works on the subject was *The Profit Magic of Stock Transaction Timing*, by J.M. Hurst. He used a type of mathematics developed by the French mathematician Fourier. Fourier's method shows how any curve can be broken down into the sum of a long series of cycle waves of specific frequencies.

I never found that this approach worked well or produced a result that was particularly useful. I decided to approach the question from another angle, using a concept from physics called resonance. I thought of

FIGURE 8.3 Analysts have often talked about a $4\frac{1}{3}$-year business and stock market cycle. The evidence for it is readily seen in this chart.

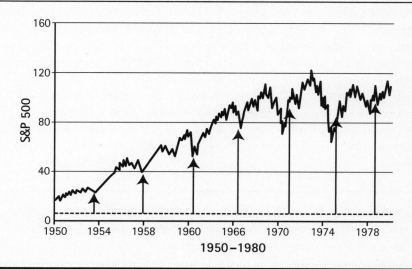

a way that moving averages might be able to locate natural cycles in the market, if they existed.

Using Resonance to Find the Time Cycles in the Market

Some physicists have speculated that resonance may have caused the walls of Jericho to fall. If an object has a natural frequency of vibration, when you push it back and forth with some force at that same frequency, you get a very large effect—that is *resonance*. With resonance, the object vibrates to an extent way out of proportion to the cause of the vibration. The frequency of the force must be close to the natural frequency of the object; if the force vibrates at other frequencies, you get a much smaller effect. In the story of Jericho, presumably, the sound frequency of the enemy's trumpets matched the natural frequency of the walls, causing them to vibrate wildly and fall apart.

Another example of resonance is found in a tuning fork, which has a specific vibration frequency. Strike it and you hear a tone. If you play music near a tuning fork, the tuning fork vibrates not only at its natural frequency, but also at the different frequencies of the music. However, by far the biggest vibration in the fork results when the frequency of the music is exactly equal to the tuning fork's natural frequency. Other frequencies make it vibrate, but much less so.

Figure 8.4 shows the standard mathematical curve that indicates when resonance is occurring. The graph displays how much a tuning fork, for example, vibrates when you apply different frequencies of music (or notes) to it. The largest movement of the tuning fork occurs when the frequency of the sound striking the fork equals its natural frequency. This basic pattern will be important when we get to the results of the studies.

If the stock market has certain natural frequencies, how do you force the market to vibrate at different frequencies, to test for resonance as you would with a tuning fork? You can't really do that, but you can do something very similar. You can take the price curve of the S&P 500 for

---

Resonance is an unusually large vibration of a system produced in response to an external stimulus of the same frequency (or nearly the same) as the system's natural vibration frequency.

FIGURE 8.4 A system that has resonance produces this type of curve. The natural frequency of the system is at the peak of the curve.

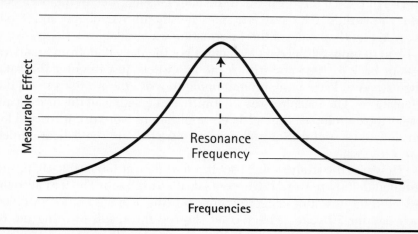

the last 70 years and see what happens when you apply different moving averages to determine which one produced the greatest profit. Trying every moving average is like trying to force the market to respond to different time frequencies. If there are natural frequencies to the market, moving averages close to those frequencies would probably be in better "harmony" with the market's price movements than moving averages of different time spans. The right moving average would catch any natural price movements closer to the bottom and closer to the top than other moving averages.

The Original Moving-Average Study

The purpose of the first study of moving averages was to answer two questions:

1. Which moving average was the best at confirming a market trend?
2. Do stock prices manifest the phenomenon known as resonance?

I did my original study in 1983, repeating it in 1992 and again in 1999. The results haven't changed since the first study.

What has changed is the availability of data and the ease of computing. I did the first study in 1983 right after I purchased one of the original IBM PCs. To do it, I needed the daily closing price of the S&P 500 from the earliest data available, plus the monthly dividend and T-bill rates. At that time none of this information was available on floppy discs, so I had to input all the data by hand. I got the daily data from Standard & Poor back to 1928 and it took me two weeks just to enter the data. Then I had to learn basic programming to write the routines to do the calculations. The machine was so slow that calculating all the moving averages took a full day. Spreadsheets applications were primitive and far too slow to be useful. Now, all that has changed and the data are much easier to obtain.

How was the study done? I set the start date at January 1, 1929, and assumed that there were 196 accounts with $1 in each. The first account reflected the result of using the 5-day moving average on the S&P 500 each day for 70 years. The second showed the result of using the 6-day moving average on the S&P 500 each day for 70 years, and so forth. The 196th account reflected the result of using the 200-day moving average.

When a moving average was positive, meaning that the closing price of the S&P 500 was above the moving average, that account was assumed to be invested in the S&P 500 (the trend was up). Any dividends declared while invested would be included and compounded. When the S&P 500 closed below the moving average, the computer sold the S&P 500 in that account and the funds went into a T-bill account to gather daily interest. As long as the price stayed below the moving average, the account stayed invested in the T-bill. When the closing price of the S&P 500 again moved above the corresponding moving average, the computer moved the account back into the S&P 500. I monitored each of the 196 accounts daily, watching how the initial $1 grew over 70 years.

The Results

Before we study how well this mechanical way of using moving averages performed, we must first establish what the S&P 500 would have produced without any changes, if one had stayed fully invested. During the 70 years under study, buying and holding the S&P 500, with dividends reinvested, produced an average return of 10.3% per year. This basic return is the benchmark against which to compare the performance of the various moving averages. The benchmark return of 10.3% is represented by the horizontal dotted line in Figure 8.5.

On the same chart, I've plotted the average yearly gain of each moving-average account produced in 70 years. For example, over 70 years, the 5-day moving average produced an average return of 8.8% per year, the 6-day a return of 8.5%, the 7-day a return of 8.2%, and so forth. I've plotted each of these results from 5 to 200 days and the other line in the figure represents the plotting of these moving-average returns. The 5-day is on the far left and the 200-day on the far right.

This chart shows that using shorter-term moving averages produces a lower return than simply buying and holding the S&P 500 average. But longer-term moving averages seem to do better than buy-and-hold—as much as 2% better. The basic pattern was what I had hoped. Although the highest point was at the 134-day moving average, resonance appears

FIGURE 8.5 Moving-average timing versus S&P 500 buy and hold. This chart shows the back-tested result of using different moving-average timing methods on the S&P 500 over 70 years (1929 to 1998). The study assumes the free-exchange privilege and that the exchange was done the day after a signal was given. The results shown are those of a variation on the normal moving average in which each moving average was shifted downward by 1.5%.

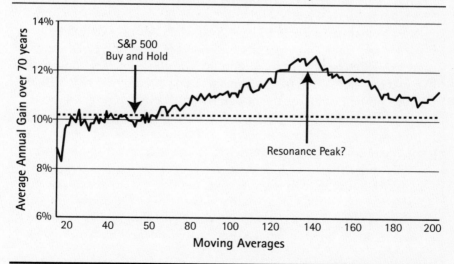

Original Study Restrictions

When I first did this study in 1983, I imposed certain restrictions to conform to the investment vehicles available at the time. I did this so that if one wanted to apply the results of the study, it would be possible. In 1983, it was possible to invest in the S&P 500 only through an index mutual fund. The spiders and exchange traded funds (ETFs) of today were not available. One disadvantage of this method is that when you buy or sell, you are limited to getting the closing price at the end of the day. Even if you decide to sell a mutual fund in the morning, you still get the price of the S&P 500 at the close of that day.

Therefore, I put this restriction in the study: The price you buy or sell at is always *the next day's price after a signal is given*. This is necessary because you have to wait until the market closes to do the new moving-average calculation. If a signal is given, your trade can't be executed until the next day, at which time the next day's *closing price* will apply.

One advantage of a mutual fund is that you can use the free-exchange privilege it provides. The free exchange allows an investor to move from the stock fund into a money market fund and back again without paying a commission. You also avoid paying the spread, which is the difference between the bid and the asking price. Some funds put restrictions on the number of times you can make such a transfer, but with the longer-term moving averages, the number of exchanges is minimized, so this would not be a problem.

It is very difficult to calculate the effects of taxes on a timing strategy. Nevertheless, it is an important consideration and one that should be carefully analyzed. Even if a timing strategy did better than a buy-and-hold strategy, the opposite might be true if taxes were factored in. Therefore, in my opinion it is best to implement this type of strategy in a tax-deferred account, such as a tax-deferred annuity, a tax-free (Roth) IRA, or a deferred retirement account or regular IRA.

The graph in Figure 8.5 shows the 70-year results of a slight variation of the simple moving averages. Besides testing every moving average, I also tested many variations of these moving averages, such as what would happen to the results if I shifted every moving average up or down a little. I tried many different shifts for every

> average, which gave me the ability to fine-tune each one, much like going back and forth on a radio dial helps find the exact point of best reception.
>
> Figure 8.5 reflects this fine-tuning. I obtained the best results by shifting all the moving averages downward by 1.5%. In other words, the decision to move in or out of the S&P 500 was whether the S&P 500 was higher or lower than 98.5% of the moving average. This fine-tuning helped push the peak point to its maximum.

to peak at the 130-day moving average, which produced an average return of 12.5%, about 2% better than the average S&P 500 buy-and-hold result over the 70-year period examined.

The 130-Day Moving Average

After calculating and plotting the 70-year results, I looked very carefully at the high point: the 130-day moving average. Although it wasn't the moving average that produced the absolute highest return (that was the 134-day moving average), it was the center point of the curve if I smoothed it out and rounded it over. Using the 130-day moving average, I plotted the day-to-day result that led to a 12.5% average annual return and compared it to the daily buy and hold result of the S&P 500. Figure 8.6 shows the daily growth of $1 using this adjusted 130-day moving average plotted against the growth of $1 in the S&P 500.

The original study covered a long period and many types of markets. A number of people have questioned whether it is actually a worthwhile measure since the structure of the market has changed over time, as has the economy. This is true, but the human factor in trading probably overrides or mitigates the effects of these structural changes. Any market reaction to emotional trading that would produce certain repetitious cyclical movements would still stand out over such a long period. In other words, if a cycle existed for only a short period, the long period of the study would have washed it out and not have highlighted any particular moving average.

FIGURE 8.6   Best moving-average result versus S&P 500. I chose the 130-day moving average (downshifted 1.5%) and calculated the resulting daily value over 70 years. This graph compares that daily value to the daily value of buying and holding the S&P 500.

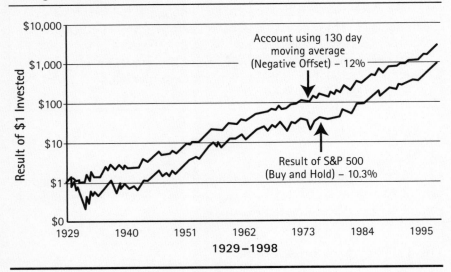

Since the 70 years included the Great Depression, two long (18-year) bull markets, and a 16-year trading range, this study presents a timing method that seems to work well over a long period and through markets of all types. Some might consider using the 130-day moving average a panacea: The theoretical results are better than buy and hold and it allows one to avoid major bear markets. However, it's not a panacea. One major problem with using any moving average to determine the trend is the phenomenon known as the whipsaw.

Factoring in the Whipsaw

For all their uses, moving averages present potentially frustrating and costly drawbacks. The whipsaw is the major one. A *whipsaw* occurs when the price rises above the moving average, signaling a buy into the market, and then reverses, causing an exchange backout, during which you often end up selling at a lower price than you just paid. It is important to un-

A **whipsaw** is a quick reversal in a moving-average signal. When the price gets close to the moving average, it can at times move above and below the moving average many times before it firmly establishes a trend. These movements produce a false confirmation of the trend and a false signal to buy or sell. Whipsaws cause you to buy high and sell low most of the time, and normally two out of three signals using moving averages produce a negative return. Whipsaws can be very extreme in volatile markets and can erode gains. As far as I know, there is no way to avoid them.

derstand that when using moving averages, approximately two-thirds of all exchanges end with a negative result, and it is probably unavoidable.

Yet these studies also indicate that even with the erosion from whipsaws, a well-planned trend-following method can work well over many market cycles. If the moving average is chosen carefully, the advantage of participating in all the major market advances and being out of all the major declines outweighs the alternative of buying and holding over long periods, *even when losses from whipsaws are factored in*. Back-testing through all types of markets would appear to confirm this assertion.

Another fact becomes obvious after studying Figure 8.6: During long advancing markets, such as the ones from 1949 to 1966 and from 1982 until 2000, almost any trend-following technique underperforms the simple buy-and-hold strategy. During these periods, the declines are seldom big enough to produce a benefit by trying to time them, and the whipsaws erode the results. The gain using moving averages occurs primarily in a negative way, by avoiding the major declines. At these times, trend following adds value by allowing the investor to avoid giving the gains back during severe declines. We can see how trend following using moving averages would begin to make sense during an extended trading-range market, such as the one I think we've entered.

You can see all this in Figure 8.6. As just said, the buy-and-hold strategy does better than moving average strategies during long bull markets (1949 to 1968 and 1982 to 1999), but the moving average strategy gains substantially on buy and hold during corrective periods. It seems that the sum total of the whipsaws—losing during long bull markets but gaining during certain declines—adds up to an overall positive result for a carefully planned trend-following method.

The original study, besides presenting this interesting result, introduces you to the concept of timing using moving averages. It shows the basic method of testing how they work and how to display and compare the results. This prepares you for the new study, which focused not on the whole 70 years, but on the last major trading range—the 16.5-year period from 1966 to 1982. What moving-average strategies would have worked the best through just that period?

THE NEW MOVING-AVERAGE STUDY

In the original 70-year study, the 130-day moving average performed best. This 70-year period was actually composed of four separate market periods: the Great Depression, the 20-year post-WWII bull market, a long 16-year sideways period (1966 to 1982), and the latest 18-year bull market. Through all these types of markets, the 130-day moving average did very well.

Price declines during bear markets were big enough and long enough for the 130-day moving average to fit within the movements, causing selling close enough to the top and buying close enough to the bottom to gain on the market. Nevertheless, the important point to note is that the 130-day moving average was not optimized for any particular type of market, it just did the best over the whole period. Therefore, we don't know if the 130-day moving average would be the best one to use if we thought the market was about to enter a long trading range period.

The 1966 to 1982 Period

Figure 8.7 shows the S&P 500 from 1950 through 1982, with the period from 1966 to 1982 highlighted. Between the years 1966 and 1982, the market moved back and forth in a broad trading range (although the S&P 500 doesn't show it as clearly as the Dow does, the consensus is that the postwar bull market ended in 1966 when the Dow hit 1,000). I believe we are entering a similar trading range period but with a much smaller time frame, from 5 to 7 years. This previous period, however, might provide a good testing ground for moving-average strategies that might work the best through a trading range period.

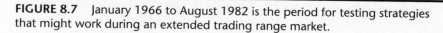

FIGURE 8.7   January 1966 to August 1982 is the period for testing strategies that might work during an extended trading range market.

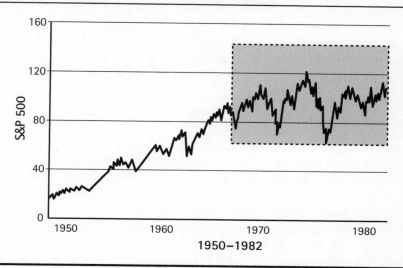

Adding More Dimension to Moving Averages

The research task is simple: Test every moving average just as before, but limit the period to 1966 to 1982. These moving averages aren't magical; they don't predict the economic situation or the market. They are used only as a trend-defining mechanism. The goal is to determine which moving average defines or catches the best trends of the market during the most recent extended trading range.

I could have performed the new study in the simple way just described, but I also wanted to test a new idea at this time. Remember that the moving average trend method always gives signals after a top or bottom. If you don't get in at the bottom or out near the top, you often miss a large part of a move. If the price moves during the trading range are not large, these misses could be important. In addition, back-and-forth movements of the market might increase the number of whipsaws. Therefore, it is worthwhile to find a strategy that also tries to locate tops and bottoms of the trading ranges.

The problem is that you know where the tops and bottoms of a range are only after the range has existed for a while. What if, by careful mathematical selection, it were possible to find the approximate tops and bottoms in past trading-range stock markets? A strategy might then be set up in anticipation of a similar type of movement. I reasoned that the best chance of finding these past extremes might be a technical tool called Bollinger bands.

Bollinger Bands

The best way to explain Bollinger bands is to show them to you. You can define a set of Bollinger bands for every moving average. Figure 8.8 shows a set of Bollinger bands for a moving average of 132 days (why I chose 132 days will become evident later). The moving average is the center line, with Bollinger bands above and below. Each band is equidistant from the moving average. Notice that at times the two bands move closer to each other and at other times they separate. How are these bands determined and why does this happen?

Sometimes the stock market becomes very active and prices move around a lot. At other times, prices can become tame and move slowly. This is volatility. We measure volatility according to *standard deviation*, a mathematical measure of how far above or below a moving average prices move. Bollinger bands are calculated using this standard deviation. When volatility is high, the top and bottom bands separate, giving the market more room to fluctuate. When volatility is low, the bands come together, allowing for less price change. Bollinger bands are good candidates for a mathematical cutoff to define the tops and bottoms of price ranges. Bollinger bands aren't fixed; they allow the top and bottom of a range to adjust as stock market conditions change.

At John Bollinger's Web site (www.bollingerbands.com), his example of Bollinger bands uses two standard deviations as the separation be-

---

Bollinger bands are a mathematical technique developed by market technician John Bollinger that uses market volatility (standard deviation) to produce two bands, or lines, that bracket a price movement. Each moving average has its own set of bands.

FIGURE 8.8   Sample of Bollinger bands. These bands, developed and popularized by market technician John Bollinger, may be a great tool for bracketing a trading range if one believes the market has entered such a period (buy at the low band and sell at the high band). The bands shown are those of the 132-day moving average using a 2s factor (twice the standard deviation).

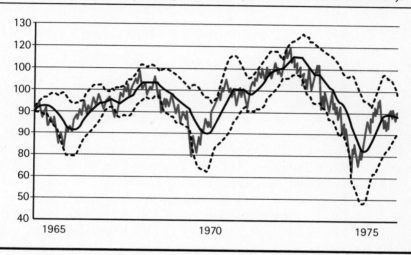

tween the moving average and the top and bottom bands. In fact, the separation of the two lines could be at any multiple of the standard deviation. In my study, I tested every possible multiple of separation and found that the two-standard-deviation bands, as John Bollinger defined them, worked very well.

Which Bollinger Band Is Best?

We know that each moving average has its own unique set of Bollinger bands. Shorter-term moving averages have tight bands that rapidly expand and contract with changes in short-term volatility, better suited to determining short-term market swings. Longer-term moving averages have wider, more stable bands, best suited for determining possible tops and bottoms of longer-term swings. If one is looking to trade market swings, is it better to trade short-, intermediate- or long-term swings of the market? This is similar to asking the question in the original study of which moving average did the best.

I hypothesized that the feedback-loop components in the model for stock prices would cause certain size-price movements to repeat just enough so that a particular Bollinger band would catch the tops and bottoms of the move better than others. The new study would establish two things:

1. Which moving average did the best between 1966 and 1982 (like the original study)
2. Which Bollinger band method of defining market tops and bottoms did the best from 1966 to 1982

It must be understood that the two strategies being tested are distinct and different. The first question would be answered by doing a study like the original. The second question, testing the various Bollinger bands to try to catch tops and bottoms, required a little more thought.

One of the limitations of using Bollinger bands as I intended to do is that if prices reach the top of the band and I sell the S&P 500, there is no obvious strategy for when to buy again. Do I wait until I get to the bottom band before I buy back in? That wasn't feasible; prices quite often didn't return to the bottom band for some time. Sell-offs after reaching the top band were often mild and wouldn't decline enough to reach the bottom band.

The Bollinger Band Strategy

The new study was set up to test every moving average between 5-day periods and 200-day periods, just like the original study. Each moving average would start with $1, and the study would keep track of the value of that dollar every day. Each moving average would be tested as it was in the original study, but I added this nuance from the Bollinger band concept: When a price reached the top Bollinger band for a given moving average, the computer would sell some of the money and put it in a T-bill account; the other money would be carried forward following the normal moving-average method.

The money that was sold out when the top band was penetrated would sit in a T-bill account until the price went below the moving average; then the remaining money would also go into the T-bill account as the normal moving-average strategy demands. At that point, 100% of the money would be in the T-bill account. If prices moved back up above the moving average, 100% of the money would be moved back into the

S&P 500—in other words, all the money would now move according to the moving-average strategy.

What would happen if prices were to go way down and penetrate the lower Bollinger band? The computer would take some of the money out of the T-bill account and buy the S&P 500 on the assumption that prices may have reached the bottom of a trading range and it might be a good time to buy. The situation would stay this way (some money invested and some still in T-bills) until prices again move above the moving average. At that point, the other money would go into the S&P 500, following the normal moving-average procedure. If prices go under the moving average again, all 100% would come out of the S&P 500 and go back into T-bills as usual.

Summarizing the Trading Range Study

In this study, I tracked two pools of money over the 16.5 years. One pool, *Strategy 1,* followed the moving-average strategy. The other, *Strategy 2,* followed the moving-average strategy except at certain moments, when Bollinger bands were penetrated, and then it followed its own signals. Preliminary studies of many combinations indicated that a good mix occurred when the Strategy 1 pool contained 60% of the assets and Strategy 2 contained 40%.

Strategy 1

Test every moving average between 5 and 200 days, including 8 vertical shifting variations up and down per moving average. I tested 1,755 moving averages. For each moving average, the strategy was to buy the S&P 500 at the close when the S&P 500 closed above the moving average, and to sell the S&P 500 at the close when the S&P 500 closed below the moving average, with the funds going into a T-bill account, as in the original study.

Strategy 2

Test Bollinger bands that are twice the standard deviation away from their moving average. I tested 1,755 Bollinger bands, one set for each of the moving averages. In Strategy 2, when the S&P 500 went above the top Bollinger band, the S&P 500 was sold and the money put into a T-bill account. It stayed there until prices either went below and then above the moving average or until the lower Bollinger band was penetrated. At these times, the money was again invested in the S&P 500. In Strategy 2, when the S&P 500 went below the lower Bollinger band, the S&P 500 was purchased. It stayed invested in the S&P 500 until prices either went above and then below the moving average or until the upper Bollinger band was penetrated. At these times, the S&P 500 was sold and the money put into a T-bill account.

Restrictions on the New Study

Since the original moving-average study, new investment vehicles have been developed that overcome one of its major limitations: having to accept the next-day closing price after a signal is given on the market's close. When I did the original study, it wasn't feasible—or even possible—to calculate the moving average right up to the end of the trading day and then to execute the free exchange before the market closed.

With current computer systems, however, you can know the value of the S&P 500 minute by minute, right up to the close. There also are Spyders (representing one share of stock in the S&P 500) and programmed trading methods (for institutions) for buying and selling baskets of stock that mirror the S&P 500 at any minute. For the new study, therefore, I decided to assume the capabilities that these new trading vehicles might allow.

I assumed that I could monitor the condition of the moving average and the Bollinger bands right up to the close. If a signal were given, the assumption was that the price of buying or selling the S&P 500 would be the closing price for the same day. In practice, this might be difficult to do if the moving average or the Bollinger bands were very close to the price at the close, but I think it would be possible in most cases.

These new ways of investing in the S&P 500 would change one of the earlier assumptions. Previously I had assumed that there was no transaction cost since I would use the free-exchange privilege of the index mutual fund. Since the study now assumes that Spyders are being bought or sold, a transaction cost for a round-trip transaction must be added. The spread, or price difference, between the *bid* and the *ask* was also assumed. For the study, I assumed a round-trip expense cost to buy and sell, which included commissions and the spread between the bid and ask prices, of 35 basis points, which is 35/100 of 1%.

I cannot present the entire study here because it is too detailed. Although the study identified several good strategies, I'm going to show you just one of the most successful results (Figure 8.9).

As in the first study, the benchmark is the total return of the S&P 500 during this 16-year period: 5.06%. In Figure 8.9, this buy-and-hold return is shown as the dotted line. The other line plots the average annual return each moving average produced (maintaining an asset mix of 60% moving average and 40% Bollinger band). The two moving averages that are highlighted are the 72-day and the 132-day. Both produced back-tested average returns of just over 10, which is 5% more than the S&P buy-and-hold strategy produced. The chart also seems to indicate

FIGURE 8.9 The 1966 to 1982 study. The line at the bottom shows the S&P 500 buy-and-hold strategy. In a sideways market, the two 72-day and 132-day moving averages did pretty well. The study used two concurrent strategies: 60% of the assets followed the moving-average signal and 40% followed the Bollinger band strategies. These results reflect a variation of the simple moving average. In this study, better results occurred when the moving averages were raised upward on the price scale by 1%, which is the opposite of what was discovered in the 70-year study. The assumption here was buying and selling the S&P 500 Spyders and using the price on the S&P 500 at the close of the day the moving-average signal was given. A 35-basis-point allowance was used for the spread and the commission.

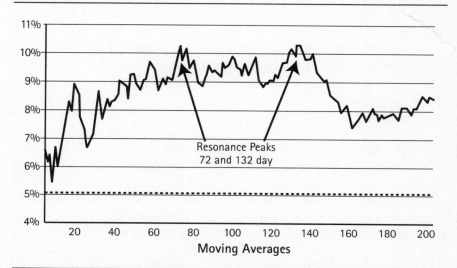

that almost any market-timing method works better than buy and hold through long trading range markets.

In the earlier study, I tested a number of variations on moving averages by adjusting the moving average line up and down, searching for a relationship that would improve the moving-average returns. The curve in Figure 8.9 plots one of the variations that produced a good result. This variation resulted from shifting all the moving averages upward by 1%. In other words, I calculated the moving average and then multiplied it by 1.01, which raised the moving average on the price axis. It had the effect of generating sell signals earlier and buy signals later.

I decided to focus on two moving averages from this study, the 72-day moving average and the 132-day moving average. It is important to note that moving averages around 130 days worked well in almost all studies of various market periods. They worked the best for the entire 70-year study *and* for the 16.5-year sideways market. The difference was only in the shift: In 70 years, the 130-day moving average shifted downward 1.5%, and in the sideways period, the shift was upward by 1%.

The Results

I have always found it easier to visualize how these strategies performed by looking at the day-to-day result of each moving average. Figure 8.10 shows the day-by-day result of the 132-day moving-average strategy (60% Strategy 1 and 40% Strategy 2), and Figure 8.11 shows the 72-day results (also 60% Strategy 1 and 40% Strategy 2), both plotted against the S&P 500 buy and hold.

It's easy to see from these figures how the strategies work. The moving averages and their Bollinger bands provided a good time measure to catch the major upward moves early while sidestepping most of the declines and allowing the Bollinger bands to catch the extremes of the movements.

Because both moving averages (132-day and 72-day) gave consistent returns and each gave a better than 10% average annual return for the 16.5-year period, I decided that a combined strategy using both moving averages would probably perform the best. An average of the two would produce about the same total return as either one alone, but the path to get there would be smoother for the same reason we diversify in portfolio theory (i.e., when one investment zigs, the other zags). The total return for combining the 72-day and the 132-day moving averages 50 : 50

FIGURE 8.10 Plotting the day-by-day value of the 132-day result (moving average and Bollinger band) versus the daily S&P 500 buy and hold.

132-Day Bollinger Band and Moving-Average Strategy Study
1966–1982

FIGURE 8.11 Plotting the day-by-day value of the 72-day result (moving average and Bollinger band) versus the daily S&P 500 buy and hold.

72-Day Bollinger Band and Moving-Average Strategy Study
1966–1982

TABLE 8.1   Yearly results of the combined 72- and 132-day moving-average strategies from 1966 to 1982

Year	S&P 500	Combined 72 and 132
1966	–10.1%	–0.1%
1967	23.9%	19.3%
1968	15.5%	13.7%
1969	–9.2%	4.6%
1970	2.2%	18.0%
1971	15.4%	17.8%
1972	19.4%	7.3%
1973	–14.8%	1.6%
1974	–26.7%	–4.5%
1975	34.1%	21.0%
1976	22.9%	14.8%
1977	–7.2%	0.8%
1978	6.6%	12.6%

was 10.3% per year from 1966 to July 1982. Table 8.1 shows the combined yearly results.

MOVING AVERAGES AND FEEDBACK LOOPS

Recall from Chapter 1 the stock market model that says the price of stocks equals a fair value modified and stretched by the action of three feedback loops. These loops are generated by the emotional reaction of investors focusing on three separate time frames. The conclusions from these moving-average studies seem to show that these feedback loops, once started, tend to continue for specified periods. In other words, the economic factors (fair value) can change as the economy changes, but the one constant—the human being and his or her reaction to events—is nearly the same through all eras. These reactions create the recurring cycles that moving averages measure.

The moving averages that did the best in the study seem to be the ones that fit or harmonized with how groups of investors react and create market movements as feedback loops. As stated before, these feedback loops can run for a maximum of about 13 weeks down or about 26 weeks up. The 132-day and 72-day moving averages fit in the time scale we would expect of feedback loop movements.

Will this change over time? After all, there were only 400 mutual funds in the mid-1970s, and now there are over 10,000; the market seems more complex than it used to be. Today the Internet allows people to trade on a daily basis for a small commission. It would seem that the relative number of investors in the three time realms—short-term, intermediate-term, and long-term—is not a constant but is changing, maybe significantly. Won't this modify the size of the various feedback-loop movements and their relationships, disturbing the ways these time realms interacted in the past? I believe it will have an effect, but it is difficult to anticipate exactly what that effect will be.

The increase in day trading should modify the short-term feedback loops; perhaps that will set into motion more intermediate-term moves. The definite increase in short-term price volatility reflects the larger number of traders who trade for short periods. (In other words, the short-term feedback loop has been magnified.) My hope is that the 72-day and 132-day moving averages are long enough to smooth away some of these changes and will still work.

USING STANDARD TECHNICAL ANALYSIS

There will be other ways to try to invest through a period like the one I'm expecting. Besides using the strategies presented in this chapter, standard technical and fundamental analysis and the lessons we learned during the 1970s and 1980s will be very important. Much of this information is summarized in the indicators and ideas presented in Chapters 4 and 5. These ideas cannot be back-tested as thoroughly as the methods shown in this chapter, but the good track records of some market technicians who actually navigated the stock market of the 1970s show the potential of this knowledge.

My principle of time invariance says that if an idea is useful for locating an intermediate-term top or bottom, the same principle is useful for locating short-term tops and bottoms. The only difference is that the time scale of measurement should be reduced to reflect the different time domain of interest. It will be important to remember this during the upcoming period.

Of the various technical tools available, I cannot overemphasize how important market sentiment will be at locating the intermediate tops and bottoms that will make up the trading ranges of this period. The long, successful records of investment recommendations by Robert Farrell,

Martin Zweig, Bob Schaeffer, and Joseph Granville are attributable to a great degree on their use of contrary opinion indicators.

Although I believe the near future will essentially be a trading range period for the overall stock market, certain groups of stocks will outperform others. A trading range market will apply for most stocks, but a bull market—albeit a slow-moving and undramatic one—will be in force for a number of other stocks and for select groupings. The task is to identify these *stealth bull markets*, as I like to call them. Only after looking back over 2- or 3-years will we be able to separate the trading range groups from those that have been slowly advancing over the period. These particular segments will appear to be in a trading range, but in reality they will be trading ranges with a distinct upward bias that will become clear only after a number of years.

For example, there will be a time to buy technology stocks again. In early 2000, I wrote the following.

> I believe that before this trading range correction is over, a complete reversal in the extreme speculation that occurred in the technology sector must occur. I think that someday we will hear a chorus arise saying, "How could we have seen so much potential and have been so wrong?" When I hear that chorus, it will be one important sign that the end of the correction is near and a new investment cycle in technology is ready to begin.

That prediction is coming true very nicely. Technology stocks will again rise out of the ashes—when the investment community believes there is no longer much of a future in technology.

The change will not be dramatic but will slowly emerge. Prices will begin a gradual but constant rise, causing little commotion or attention. We are rapidly approaching that point, and it happened a lot faster than I had projected when prices were at their peak. I had expected that it would take about 4 years to squeeze the speculative excesses out of the technology sector. The market is indicating that it will happen faster than that.

THE RISE OF HEDGE FUNDS

Hedge funds are a very misunderstood investment form. This is unfortunate because hedge funds will offer investors a new way to make money during a trading range market. It will take a lot of re-education to overcome the misconceptions.

Why Mutual Funds Might Not Do as Well

I remember at the end of 1982 that the 10-year performance numbers of mutual funds were dismal. At least half of the funds posted negative returns during the decade, which meant that most mutual fund investors who had held funds for 10 years made little if any money. Sixteen years later, by 1998, over half the mutual funds were reporting 10-year performance numbers exceeding 20% per year—accounts increasing more than four and five times in value.

Had the mutual fund money managers become that much better at picking stocks over the 16 years between 1972 and 1998? Of course not. This situation simply reflects what we discussed in Chapter 2, that any large, diversified group of stocks will behave much like the market. The negative 10-year fund numbers between 1972 and 1982 simply reflect the fact that the stock market, as measured by broad stock indices, was in a trading range. The high returns from 1988 to 1998 were simply a reflection of skyrocketing stock prices. This means that most of the return from stock mutual funds doesn't originate from the skill of the money manager but from the natural return from stocks over the period in question. If we are entering another trading range market, mutual funds as a class will very likely give correspondingly bad results, just as they did between 1972 and 1982.

Mutual funds invest according to the mandate of their prospectus—the legal document that describes their investment goals, the type of investments they can use, and a little about their strategy. Most funds cannot sell short the market to any great degree and, in fact, SEC law puts a restrictive upper limit on this practice. Mutual funds are primarily a bull market investment vehicle. They also have certain turnover limits. Mutual fund money managers aren't supposed to become short- or intermediate-term traders or to hold high cash positions if they are nervous about stock prices. History has shown that mutual fund managers increase cash in bear markets, but few increase it to a high level. The mutual fund cash position has never exceeded 15% for mutual funds as a group, even during the worst 2-year bear market of the last 40 years. Mutual funds are not designed to trade a trading range market.

As I explained in Chapter 5, it fits within my understanding of contrary opinion to have the general return from mutual funds fall off sharply in the coming years. After all, the last 10 years have witnessed the largest explosion in mutual fund assets in our history. The influx of investor money has been enormous. In a sense, contrary opinion says that when this carries to such an extreme, investors will get the opposite of what they expected; if so, investors are going to be disappointed in their returns, and this flow of money into mutual funds will soon reverse, as investors start looking for other ways to earn money. A flat U.S. market will probably also bring about flatter world stock prices. There will be bull markets in some countries, but if the U.S. stock market enters a trading range, other countries' stock markets probably will, too. Investors throughout the world will be facing the same or similar problems. To overcome this, I believe investors will start turning their attention to hedge funds.

Hedge Funds

Hedge funds are grossly misunderstood. Most people think hedge funds are risky, yet hedge funds often use strategies that are less risky than most mutual funds. One of the problems here originates in language, and it is the same problem as with the term *mutual funds*. Someone might say that mutual funds are risky but a government-guaranteed, T-bill, money market fund is a mutual fund. We classify both this T-bill money market fund and a high-risk Internet fund as mutual funds, but their risk levels are completely different as mutual funds. The common factor is not the risk of the investment, it is that they follow the same laws and rules required of a mutual fund.

The same is true of hedge funds. Many hedge funds are as different from one another as night and day, but they are similar in one respect: They must follow certain common legal and administrative rules demanded of hedge funds by the SEC.

Since a hedge fund can execute investment strategies that are restricted for mutual funds, the SEC wants to make sure that a hedge fund doesn't become a mutual fund in disguise. Therefore, unlike mutual funds, which have no shareholder limits, U.S. hedge funds are limited regarding the number of investors to a maximum of either 99 or 499, depending on a number of criteria. Furthermore, not everyone can invest in hedge funds even if they want to. Each investor must be *accredited*, which means that each investor has either a specific high net worth or annual income.

The rules also prevent hedge funds from advertising. It's as if the government is saying, "You can exist outside the normal mutual fund regulatory arena and do your nonstandard investment strategies, but only under strict conditions." Another feature of hedge funds, not allowed with mutual funds, is that the money manager can participate in the earnings of the fund. In other words, the hedge fund manager's earnings can include a certain percentage of the gain in the fund. This is strictly prohibited in mutual funds.

A hedge fund is an investment vehicle that commingles investors' money in one fund, follows the SEC requirements for hedge funds, and uses a variety of investment strategies and investment types. In my opinion, unlike a mutual fund, a hedge fund's investment return depends much more on the skill of the manager and not so much on the natural return for stocks, bonds, and so forth. This is exactly what is required in a trading range market.

Expected Rising Popularity of Hedge Funds

I believe the next 5 years will see a large increase in interest in and popularity of hedge funds. I make this prediction based on the following.

- The number of accredited investors has exploded. The stock market advance has thrown more and more people over the $1 million mark for net worth. Ten years ago, only about 0.3% of the population was accredited; now this percentage is well over 1%.
- The low return from mutual funds during a trading range market will spur investors to start looking around for alternatives. This will induce a learning cycle to understand more about these alternative methods of investing. Hedge funds are often called alternative investments.
- If the stock market experiences the decline in volatility I'm expecting (as outlined in Chapter 7), there will be an interest in other markets with greater volatility and the potential to produce stronger investment returns. Currencies, gold and silver, oil, and other investments will be considered. Some of these other markets are best tapped through some type of hedge fund, not through a mutual fund.

If these observations are correct, it will be important for investors to learn a lot more about this expanding investment area.

Hedge Fund Investment Strategies

The expansion in financial products (futures and options in world stock and bond indices and currencies) has increased the variety of ways a money manager can try to profit from investments besides stocks and bonds. These new strategies are really just the application of some old and familiar concepts applied to these new financial products: short selling, hedging, arbitrage, and leveraging. A new addition is the use of derivatives (futures and options) in place of the actual investment. From these strategies come a number of methods that try to make money over and above the simple action of buying a portfolio of stocks or bonds. These strategies require a lot more investment skill and expertise.

Several companies evaluate the performance of hedge funds. They categorize hedge funds into types, much as mutual funds are categorized by the type of stocks or bonds they invest in. However, since hedge funds are primarily distinguished by an investment method and not by an asset class, the categories are usually types of investment strategies. For this book I have used the classification of Van Hedge Fund Advisors International, Inc. Following are the 14 strategy classifications that are commonly used to categorize hedge funds.

1. Aggressive growth
2. Distressed securities
3. Emerging markets
4. Fund of funds
5. Income
6. Macro
7. Market neutral—arbitrage
8. Market neutral—securities hedging
9. Market timing
10. Opportunistic
11. Several strategies
12. Short selling
13. Special situations
14. Value

I have chosen five of these strategies that might be particularly likely to do well during a trading range market (Figure 8.12).

1. Fund of Funds. Managers invest in a group of single-manager hedge funds or manage accounts that use a variety of invest-ing strategies, creating a diversified investment vehicle for their investors.

2. Market neutral, securities hedging. Managers invest in securities both long and short, attempting on average to have a low net market exposure. Managers generally attempt to select longs that are undervalued and shorts that are overvalued, theorizing that market volatility will be minimized.

3. Special situations. This category is also known as *event-driven investing.* Managers invest when stock and bond prices are expected to change in a short period of time due to a special situation, such as a stock buy-back, spinoff, bond upgrade, or earnings surprise, to name a few. Managers take long positions in positive situations and short positions in negative situations.

4. Opportunistic. Managers employ a variety of approaches for capital appreciation. Managers opportunistically move to asset classes or strategies that give what they feel are the best possible returns. An opportunistic manager could also be invested in many different strategies, like value, special situations, and distressed securities at one time.

5. Market timing. Managers switch among asset classes in an attempt to time various markets. Asset classes used include stocks, bonds, mutual funds, and money market funds.

FIGURE 8.12 The quarterly growth, starting at $1, of the five hedge fund categories. (Source: Van Hedge Fund Advisors International, Inc.)

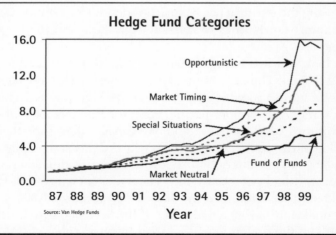

AN OPTION STRATEGY FOR TRADING RANGE MARKETS

Options on indexes such as the S&P 500 or the Dow Jones industrials are
one of the new derivative investments mentioned in Chapter 5 in the discussion of the theory of contrary opinion. I called options *bets* on
whether the stock market was going up or down. Buying a put is a bet
that prices will fall, and buying a call is a bet that prices will rise. Of
course, puts and calls are not really bets; they actually represent something real and tangible.

An *index option* is a contract between two people that exists for a
specific period (the expiration date). A *call option* is a contract that allows the owner (buyer) of that option to purchase the index at that set
price (called the *strike price*) for that entire period. If a buyer uses that
contract to purchase the index, it is said that he or she *exercised* the option. The seller of that contract must be willing to sell that index to that
buyer at the fixed price for the life of the contract. Settlements are in
cash.

There are many options on an index, defined by expiration date and
strike price. For an option in which the strike price is higher than the
value of the index at that moment, the option's actual value (called its *intrinsic value*) is zero. This should be clear because who would want to
pay more for something than it is worth? Even if an option has no intrinsic value, it will always have a time premium value. The *time premium
value* is the price given the option by speculators who are willing to buy
it now, hoping the stock or index might rise above the strike price,
thereby giving the option a true value. If it doesn't, the option price (the
time premium) slowly sinks to zero on expiration, and the buyer loses
everything.

Let's look at a real example. On July 13, 2001, the S&P 500 index
closed at 1,215.64. The call option to buy the S&P 500 at a strike price of
1,300 for the next 5 months was priced at 34 S&P points. Who would
want to exercise this option, paying 1,300 for the S&P 500 when they
could buy it for 1,215? No one would. We can see, therefore, that the intrinsic value of this option was zero. So why did it cost anything—much
less 34 points—to buy this option? Because there was time left on the option contract, it had potential value. There was a chance that the S&P
500 would start an upward move that carried it above 1,300, at which
point it would start having a real value. If the S&P 500 rose further, to a
price of 1,334, the option would have an intrinsic value of 34—exactly

what it cost on July 13. If the S&P 500 continued to go up, the option would continue to gain in value. If the S&P 500 got to 1,368, the option would be worth 64, at which point the option's original buyer would have doubled his or her investment.

That's partly why I called options bets. The buyer of an option whose index price is below the strike price is betting that over time the market will go up, eventually making the option worth something before expiration. The further one is from the strike price, the longer the odds. On the other hand, if the market rises, but much less than expected, the option will eventually go to zero as expiration nears. For example, the S&P 500 might rise from 1,215 to exactly 1,300, a gain of 7%. If it then falls back, that option will end up worthless.

On the other side of the contract, the seller of the call option that has a time premium is getting money from the sale, with the idea that he or she is selling something that has a long way to go before it actually will have a value. The seller does this under the assumption that the index would never go much above the strike price over the life of the option, or if it did, it would at least fall back and have no value on expiration.

Now let's look at a put option. The buyer of a put option has purchased the right to sell the S&P 500 at a fixed price until expiration. The seller of the put must buy it from him at that price until expiration. Let's look at July 13, 2001 again. On that date, the put option to sell the S&P 500 at a price of 1,100 for the next 5 months costs 24 S&P 500 points. The put option, like the call option in our previous example, has no intrinsic value, only time value. There was a chance, however, that the S&P 500 could start a large decline that carried it below 1,100, at which time the put would start having a real value. If the S&P 500 declined further, to a price of 1,076, the option would now have an intrinsic value of 24, just what it cost on July 13. If the S&P 500 continued to decline, the option would continue to gain in value.

A combination write is a well-known option strategy that is designed specifically for a trading range market. A *combination write* is the simultaneous selling of a put and a call with the same expiration date at two different strike prices (Figure 8.13). The seller gets the money from the buyer of these obligations. Suppose you expected that the S&P 500 would never get above 1,300 or below 1,100 over the next 5 months; you think the market will simply trade between these two extremes, going back and forth in a sawtooth pattern. As long as the S&P 500 index stays below 1,300 and above 1,100, the two options are guaranteed to expire

FIGURE 8.13   A combination write is an option strategy to use if you are expecting prices to remain in a trading range. Ideally, the put and the call should be sold when traders are putting unusually high time premiums into the options. This usually occurs when the VIX index (volatility index) is at a maximum. The assumption is that this volatility will calm down over succeeding months, and meanwhile one would have received a high price for selling the two options. As long as prices stayed within strike prices, the obligation assumed by selling the options would expire worthless.

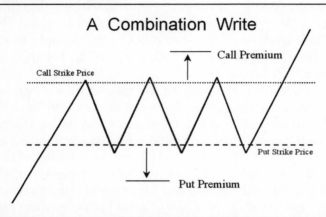

worthless. You pocket the money and let the situation go to zero. It's obvious why this is an option strategy designed for a trading range market.

Combination writes do pose risks, however. If the market breaks above or below either strike price and continues past what the seller pocketed, the speculator has taken a position that can lead to increasing losses. No one should establish a combination write without first determining a well-established stop-loss point. In other words, before the combination write is established, clear exit prices should be established at which the combination writer buys back the options and gets out from underneath the obligation at a pre-established loss. Barring such an exit strategy, if prices move above or below these strike prices and continue on that course, the buyer of a combination write could start losing on the investment, perhaps in a very big way.

A FUND OF FUNDS FOR A TRADING RANGE MARKET

It would seem that if you were expecting a trading range stock market, a fund of funds could be designed with a diversified set of hedge fund strategies that do particularly well during this type of market. The trading range strategies should be those that produce investment results in trading range markets, for example, the fund could be composed of these five hedge fund strategies.

1. Market neutral—securities hedging
2. Special situations
3. Market timing:
   - Trend following
   - Price transition indicators
4. Opportunistic
5. Option strategies

One of the advantages (or risks) of assuming that a trading range market exists is that one can set aside certain strategies that wouldn't work well during a sideways market. One of the reasons the investment results of a fund of funds don't always do so well is that the funds include every type of hedge fund strategy there is, and some of these are contradictory (i.e., they work against each other).

There is always risk. By focusing on strategies for a trading range market, if we *do* have a trading range market, a hedge fund should do very well indeed. In truth, however, we have shifted the risk to the accuracy of our prediction of a trading range market. If it doesn't materialize, the fund will not do as well as other funds. For example, if the great bull market starts up again and continues on an unrelenting advance for another six years, this strategy will probably not work as well as others.

Index